Barbara Mullen has published three previous books, *EVERY EFFORT*, St. Martin's Press, *WHEN YOU MARRY A MAN WITH CHILDREN*, Pocket Books, Simon & Schuster and *DOMINIC'S DAUGHTER*, Wheatmark Publishers. Her freelance articles have appeared in the *Boston Herald*, the *Cape Cod Times* and *Sojourner*.

She now lives in the San Francisco Bay area near her two sons, Sean and Terence, and her four grandsons, William, Christopher, Edward and Fynnigan.

UNSAFE HARBOR

Barbara Mullen

UNSAFE HARBOR

Copyright © 2012 Tenacity Press

Copyright © 2012 Tenacity Press
All rights reserved.

ISBN: 0-6156-5572-6
ISBN-13: 9780615655727

Acknowledgements

I would not have written this book without the constant encouragement, generous advice, and help from others. I would like to acknowledge some of them.

First, I want to acknowledge my late dear friend Carly who gave me valued literary advice for this book as she has for previous books over the years.

I must also give credit to the East Bay Writers Group – especially Cleo Jones, Len Smith and Travis Richardson for the hours they spent critiquing this manuscript chapter by chapter to its final version.

I want to express appreciation to Kathy Saideman, my longtime editor, and my friend Kay Baldinelli, both of whom believed in the book from the very beginning.

I offer many thanks to my family – brothers- and sisters-in-law, Bill and Pug, Floyd and Yolanda and Dan and Nancy, and to my sons Sean and Terence who supported my reasons for writing this book.

And I give special thanks to Leslie Morgan Steiner, author of *Crazy Love*, a brave memoir of surviving domestic violence, for giving me the confidence to find a publisher for *Unsafe Harbor*.

Chapter One

Carrying a large canvas bag loaded with weekend supplies, Katie hurried behind Jeff toward the parked car in the driveway. Then suddenly Jeff swung round. "What the hell is keeping you? Get the lead out of your rear," he groaned. "I wanted to have the boat well out of Barrington Harbor by now." As he jerked himself round to face forward again, a bag of groceries plummeted from his arms and splattered in Katie's path. She and her canvas bag lunged ahead onto the loose stone driveway along with tins of food, a flashlight and a carton of ice. With blood dripping down her legs, she picked herself up.

"Damn!" Jeff yelled as Katie struggled to her feet. Furiously, he started to shove the spilt items back into the paper bag and canvas carryall. "Come on. Get in the car," he said. "We can wash off the bruises on the boat."

During their drive to the harbor, Jeff kept repeating that he'd expected to be well underway by now. "I didn't know you were following me that closely. But you should know I get antsy when I'm set to go somewhere. Why can't you be more organized?"

Katie didn't know why, except that she'd felt under awful pressure since, without warning, his four kids moved in with them a year ago, three weeks after their wedding. She'd always been such a together person. Now, with Jeff, even her usual to do lists hadn't helped. Inevitably, some things didn't get done, and she could only hope they weren't vitally important to Jeff. God forbid, that one of his kids should miss an activity or an appointment, even though *he* had promised to be in charge of his kids. Uggh – time to remind him of this again. *At least he is paying a housekeeper now so I can keep my job at the newspaper,* she reminded herself. *Let him rant. Perhaps he'll get it out of his system before we board the sailboat.*

At the harbor, Katie climbed one bare foot at a time from a foot of ocean water into their dinghy. When she and Jeff had settled in the dinghy, she took a Kleenex from her pocket and dabbed at the worst bruises on her leg.

Jeff pulled the cord to start the outboard motor and turned the dinghy in the direction of their sailboat while she gazed ahead in the direction of its mooring further out in the harbor.

That summer on earlier trips to Newport and Block Island, riding seven-foot swells in a gale, dodging rocks in the fog or sunning on deck, Katie had begun to see Jeff as two separate people. As if viewing him through slanted light, she had split him in two. At sea he became her tender, loving companion; at home he remained her husband, sometimes affectionate, often difficult. She saw herself as being in a constant state of readiness, one foot perpetually raised and prepared for the quick change of direction from one version of him to the other.

She stuck her fingers over the side, cupped a handful of salt water and poured it over her knee and grimaced. An activity she and Jeff enjoyed, like sailing, ought to take precedence over others. But over what? The problem was, everything was urgent to Jeff.

"Sit down, Katie," he said when they had climbed the ladder into the cockpit. "That left knee doesn't look good. We'll have to clean it and bandage it."

He lowered his tall frame into the cabin and returned with a first-aid kit. Kneeling in front of her, he rubbed a cotton ball with disinfectant over her knee.

"Why not get ready the night before? I could buy supplies after work on Friday nights and you could pack us up after dinner," she offered.

He stretched a piece of tape over a square of gauze, touched her cheek with his finger and then brushed her long auburn hair back from her face. "Don't worry. I still adore you even when you screw up."

"I've never been a screw-up in my life before this! Never," she said while pushing the tape flat on each side of the gauze.

"That job is what's causing you to mess up, Katie," he said. "You can't remember personal things we need when your mind is elsewhere."

"Why my mind? Why not yours?"

He looked up at her from his kneeling position and, ignoring her question, patted her hand. "How about if I grade you from now on so you can improve your efforts? Today was a C+ so you see you have a long way to go."

"Sorry, I don't appreciate your humor right now, Jeff. Let's store the food and get going," she said choosing not to get into a discussion she knew she wouldn't win. As usual, he would calm down in an hour anyway and she would try to enjoy their buddy relationship on the sailboat for a couple of days.

With their wooden dinghy secured to the end of the sailboat, Jeff made his way forward to the bow to let go of their mooring. Then, rushing back to the cockpit, he turned on the auxiliary engine. "Hold the tiller tightly with both hands," he ordered as always, "and stay on course out of the harbor."

Her eyes fixed on one buoy, then the next, as she maneuvered the craft between them and toward the open sea. Daring to take her eyes off the buoys for a moment she took note of Jeff again and was comforted by his sure movements as he bounced around on deck, hoisting sailcloth and securing ropes. "We're underway," he called out finally, face lit up with the pride of it.

He hop-scotched his way back around cabin airshafts to the cockpit to relieve her at the tiller and she sprang up, found her balance, and climbed backwards down into the cabin. A few minutes later, she came up again and, leaning away from the boat's keel, carried a tray of Cokes and potato chips and set them on a locker. Offering Jeff a Coke, she settled herself on the locker alongside him.

He finished his Coke and handed her the empty bottle and took hold of the tiller with both hands. "You're on probation, mind you, but you may make a good first mate yet," he said with a broad smile. She saluted and looked over at him. With the sun on his face he looked as boyish and content as he had two years earlier when they first met in San Francisco.

The sails flapped every so often with a shifting wind and she took the tiller while Jeff, humming and whistling, got up and adjusted them to a new position. All day they took turns holding the tiller and resting on the deck in the sun.

In the late afternoon, his feet firmly planted on the deck, Jeff lowered the mainsail, staysail and the jib, hauling in yards of white nylon. He rushed back to the cockpit when he finished, took the tiller from Katie's hands and steered the thirty-six-foot, four-ton boat into a half-mile-wide cove and then to a spot where they could anchor. Minutes later, seeing him with his knees on the deck, his long back bent over the side lowering the anchor, she felt almost as secure with him as she had during their courtship.

Certain that the anchor was holding, he came back, sat next to her in the cockpit and slipped an arm around her waist. With her head on his shoulder, she let her gaze roam across the water from rocky banks at one side of the sandy beach to sloping grassy fields on the other. Reaching for his hand, she brought it to her lap, then turned and kissed him on the cheek.

As the sun went down, he got two sweaters from the cabin and together they watched the sky transform from clear blue to blue with pink swashes and on to gray. Indistinguishable voices drifted across the cove from two other boats that had come in and anchored after them. When the sky turned starry black, they went below and cooked beans and franks and toasted rolls over the flames on their butane stove.

Later, they crawled into the double V-berth, undressed beneath blankets and held one another for awhile before making love. Out here he still seemed the man she'd fallen in love with, exciting, funny, loving. Out here it was easy to enjoy him just as she had before they were married. In their home now he seemed like a balloon under too much pressure, ready to burst. She felt that his stress was affecting her too, making her feel chronically uneasy and not trusting her own instincts and judgment the way she used to.

With Jeff molded to the shape of her back after their lovemaking, the soft tinkling of metal rings brushing softly against the mast and the mellow sound of water nipping at the hull of the boat, she longed for their real life together to actually be this safe and peaceful.

* * * * * * *

On Monday morning hearing her car engine make a familiar sound like a knife being sharpened on a piece of granite, Katie slumped into her driver's seat and sighed. *Her* engine trouble was all Jeff needed to extinguish any remaining afterglow from their weekend on the high seas. "Wait Jeff," she called out, then turned to three kids in her car and told them to get in their dad's car. She slid in beside Jeff and Mathew, Tommy and Martha climbed into the back seat.

"I'm thankful you hadn't left yet," she said trying to be pleasant.

They let the kids out at their bus stop and she and Jeff drove on toward Barrington Village. He hadn't said a word since leaving home and now she wondered whether to coax him into conversation. Gazing ahead at the road, and vaguely aware that the signal light ahead had turned from yellow to red, she saw that Jeff's foot was still on the accelerator. "Jeff!" she cried out and the car screeched to a halt just before the intersection throwing her forward as far as her seat belt would allow, far enough to suck the breath out of her.

He stared straight ahead, clenching the steering wheel tightly with both hands. "Your car trouble is going to make me late," he groaned. "I have an important meeting this morning. That damn job of yours. Always getting in my way."

"You could have caused an accident." She rolled down her window and turned her face into the oncoming air. Was it her fault that her sick old car wouldn't start? Sure, she meant to get it tuned up last week, but there hadn't been time. Hell, maybe she *was* becoming a screw-up.

Giving him a quick glance she saw that his jaw jutted out defiantly now as he gazed ahead at the road. He got frazzled easily enough without her troubles adding to his frustrations. She snuck another peak at him. If he were a crystal glass he'd be shattering into a million pieces now. My God, why, after a lovely sail was he grinding his teeth? Damn, and why hadn't she gotten him to a therapist for his mood swings by now? His therapy had been her top priority months ago. But week after week he'd had excuses, waiting for Dr. so-and-so to call him back, trying to contact someone recommended by the AMA, denying that he needed help. She should have picked up the phone and called someone herself. Oh, sure, as though he would have dashed off immediately to an appointment she had made.

Thank goodness the garage had delivered her car to the newspaper that afternoon, saving her from having to call Jeff for a lift home. No point in reminding him of what had riled him up that morning. She came into the house, slipped out of her shoes, and laid down on the sofa, no need to rush dinner for her and Jeff. Eleven-year-old Martha was already in her room studying and sixteen-year-old Mathew and his thirteen year old brother Tommy had gone to a basketball game with the father of one of their friends.

Reluctantly, Katie got up and went out to the kitchen when she heard Jeff come in the back door. "You seem to be in a hurry," she said, making a quick inspection of the room at the same time. As usual, Mrs. Lewis had stacked the children's dirty dishes in the dishwasher and wiped the counters clean before leaving. "Don't you want to rest a while before eating? Or are you starved?"

He grabbed some utensils from a drawer. "Yes, I'm hungry. It would be nice to have dinner on the table for us for once." He dropped a spatula and a serving fork noisily onto the counter and then swung open the refrigerator door.

"I was thinking the same thing," she said. "I'm whipped tonight. At least the kids aren't standing around waiting to be fed the way they used to before we hired Mrs. Lewis. Reaching into a lower cabinet, Jeff rummaged through pots, came up with a heavy frying pan and plopped it onto the stove. Katie walked over and stood beside him. "I haven't seen you this anxious to cook since I first arrived in Rhode Island when we were in our little beach house. Do you have something special in mind?"

He opened the refrigerator again and grabbed a carton of eggs. "As though you care!"

She watched him numbly for a few seconds. "I don't know what's wrong with you, Jeff, but you're making me feel terrible." Then, as if in a trance, she crossed the room and picked up her purse from the counter. "I'm going to take a drive and let you wrestle with your own devils. Martha's in her room. The boys have gone out to a game."

When the back door swung shut behind her, she felt stupid, like a runaway kid all alone with nowhere to go. Whatever was eating him had started that morning. Maybe if she'd gotten her car tuned up last week. Maybe if she'd tried to leave work early and had his dinner ready when he got home tonight. Maybe...oh shit, maybe what? She got in her car and drove south on Beach Road through the village past her workplace, the historic granite and stone *Gazette* Newspaper building and a half a mile further.

Chapter Two

Katie huddled into a back booth at McDonald's with a hamburger and a Coke on a tray. Under the glare of fluorescent lights, she felt conspicuous and hoped no one from Jeff's company, International Computer, or the *Gazette* would wander in and recognize her. She unwrapped her hamburger and took a small bite. Something that very moment, the unforgiving brightness of the room, or her own weariness, seemed to be drawing sharp outlines around some truths that she'd managed to evade for a long time. Jeff hadn't fulfilled any of the promises he'd made weeks ago on their one year anniversary. Yes, he was paying Mrs. Lewis to do some cooking and laundry and cleaning chores finally, but then, Katie had hired the woman without his consent and his firing her would surely have stirred up some gossip about their marriage in the village.

Suddenly not feeling as hungry, she set her hamburger down and sipped her cola instead. She would have been happy to go on forever as they had been the summer she arrived in Rhode Island when each moment seemed precious as a feathery dandelion needing protection from the slightest breeze. Yet each day had brought her closer to autumn when the beaches would become deserted and the ocean resorts abandoned – and to the September morning when Jeff sprang out of bed and declared: "We need a home where my children can visit. This cottage won't do."

Katie recalled how she had trotted after realtors that fall, men in V-neck sweaters driving Volvos, women in bellbottom pantsuits scribbling notes onto clipboards. She had stuffed business cards into her shoulder purse in a useless effort to associate names later with houses – houses, by the way, that she couldn't imagine living in. "Why do you want so many bedrooms?" she kept asking Jeff. "Surely your children can double up on a weekend when they visit us?"

It wasn't as much the price of these houses that was bothering her as their size that was making her head spin. Forget wavy glass windows, slanted floors, other valued information she was supposed to be soaking up about these historic gems while following realtors up and down long hallways and in and out of oversized rooms, the question on Katie's mind was: *Who would take care of such a mammoth house?*

Then one morning Jeff called from his office bursting with news that he'd made an appointment for them to view "a charming three-story six bedroom nineteenth century captain's house" that he'd heard about.

Katie had protested but half an hour later found herself and Jeff rolling down a long stone drive leading to a grand old mansion in realtor Julie Pickering's car. "Ohhh!" Katie gasped upon seeing the place for the first time.

Jeff, who sat in the passenger's seat spun around and made a "Shhh!" sound while pressing his index finger to his lips.

Katie stifled a laugh. "It's the set of *Psycho*," she sputtered after the realtor had scrambled out of the car. "Norman Bates may greet us at the front door." But by the time she finished her sentence Jeff had leapt out of the car and was bouncing up the front porch stairs.

Then Katie noted with dismay how Jeff's face had lit up the second he peered through the etched glass windows of a double door entrance. Inside, Katie followed Jeff and Julie past a mahogany banister and down a hallway with high ceilings.

Pointing to the first room on the left, Julie bubbled, "This library will make a wonderful den." Then she crossed the hall and invited them into a living room through an ornate archway. Sunlight from a row of tall Victorian windows glowed yellow against white walls trimmed with yet more mahogany. A traditional brick fireplace stretched the full length of a wall at the far end of the room.

"Fantastic," Jeff exclaimed.

Astonished now by Jeff's unbridled enthusiasm, Katie continued to saunter numbly through the house behind him and Julie. Julie charged ahead in her camels' hair pantsuit ever more excitedly, her spirits lifted by an unending stream of questions from Jeff. Next she guided them through an identical archway on the other side of the hall and into a formal dining room.

"This captain must have lampooned a whole lot of whales in his time," Katie commented mostly to herself while feeling more disheartened every moment.

Having forgotten Katie entirely, Julie's full attention now was focused on Jeff as she spoke to his wide eyes and open mouth. Katie watched helplessly as the realtor took a pen from her suit coat pocket and summoned Jeff with a swoop of her arm into a wide, open country style kitchen. Julie slapped sheets of paper onto a counter to scribble numbers on and then to explain their significance to Jeff. Katie tried to interrupt Julie's monologue twice, each time insisting, "This is more home than we need." Getting no response from Julie or Jeff, Katie backed up and leaned her shoulder against a double size refrigerator. The longer she stood there, however, the more certain she became that this kitchen was closing in on her, that the house itself was trying to suffocate her. In fact succeeding, she acknowledged, because she couldn't seem to get a proper breath.

"I need air," she said on her way out of the kitchen. "I'll wait outside."

"Umm," Jeff mumbled still concentrating on Julie's clipboard.

Katie raced down the hall and through the etched glass doors, then plopped herself down at the foot of a wide oak tree and gulped a mouthful of oxygen.

Once they returned to their cottage Katie argued ferociously against buying the house, but Jeff seemed to have fallen in love with the place. The more negative she became the more rapidly he declined into a certified funk, finally going silent for the rest of the evening.

Jeff's sad face had a surprising effect on Katie reminding her of the way her father used to clam up when things didn't go his way. If he set up a monopoly game and nobody was in the mood to play, her dad would pout while staring hard and woefully down at the board. The longer he sat there the guiltier young Katie would feel until finally setting aside her homework or whatever she was doing to scoot into a chair next to him.

Katie, the number five child in the family, had sensed early on that her father would have been more than satisfied with the four children, three boys and a girl, that he already had when she arrived in the family. She tried her best to win his favor until one day she accepted a truth about her father: there was no use trying to gain his favor with a smile or a joke or a new tap dancing step. What he really needed to assure his sanity was a yard of space circling him at all times. Still, Katie had always been in awe of a father who had the power to make air heavy and to dull sunlight with the mere slump of his shoulders.

Having watched Jeff sulk for hours that evening in a way that was familiar to her, Katie exhaled a breath of relief before bedtime when finally he broke his silence. For the first time he admitted that all had not been perfect in his own childhood by telling her how much his family's small apartments in Queens had depressed him back then. "I've dreamed all my life of owning a home like this captain's house," he said, his voice cracking. Right then, Katie began to feel like an old Scrooge trying to whip a Christmas toy from the hands of a child.

Just before falling asleep that night she reached over and touched his shoulder and whispered, "I'll agree to the captain's house if you promise to hire someone to keep the place clean. People with houses like that used to have servants."

Katie shrunk further into the McDonald's booth. Thinking now how stupid she'd been not to have guessed his real motive for wanting that huge home. That drafty monster house certainly had never been part of the pre-marriage plans she and Jeff had made in San Francisco or in their cozy little Rhode Island beach house. In fact, many actions since their wedding bore no resemblance to pre-marriage agreements between them. Their financial arrangements least of all. She now had to pay all her own expenses even though she had given up a high salaried job at *New Times* magazine in San Francisco in order to marry him. And even though his present salary was now three times what she earned at the *Gazette*. And yet he balked at her demands that they share a bank account or credit card which also stuck her with paying many current household expenses.

Did he think his manhood would be jeopardized by sharing a credit card with his wife, she wondered? Or, was he, as she had begun to suspect, protecting his ability to make financial decisions without her. Like the evening he announced excitedly that he'd bought himself a private airplane for instance. Or, a few months later when he "surprised" her again with the purchase of a hundred thousand dollar thirty-six-foot sailing yacht.

Shoving the remainder of her burger aside, Katie faced a harsh truth head on. Jeff's attitude toward her had taken a three hundred and sixty degree turn since their wedding day. Before marriage, Jeff had praised her feistiness. He loved hearing how she had left her one drugstore, one movie theatre, one Kresge Dime Store town in Minnesota at eighteen and headed for San Francisco. And how she had worked days and attended college classes at night to earn a journalism degree, and six months later, got a reporter and feature writing job at *New Times* magazine. When they were dating Jeff encouraged her to publish her own women's issue magazine. "With your grit, you can do it," he'd assured her, "or for that matter, anything you decide to do." Since his children unexpectedly moved in – *unexpectedly* to Katie that is – his attitude had changed. Now it was all she could do to manage their chaotic daily lives.

Katie took a longer drink this time to wet her dry mouth. *Jeff is plowing through our rose garden with a John Deere tractor,* she admitted, asking herself: *Why didn't I listen to my old pal Maxine in San Francisco?*

"Jeff gives me a twitchy feeling down my spine," Maxine had told Katie after meeting him the very first time. "He couldn't seem to lock eyes with me." Then, swinging her long blonde hair to one side, Maxine had added, "I see the look on your face. 'That old saw' you're thinking."

"Maybe he was ashamed at having murdered both his parents with a pick axe," Katie had answered. "Shit, Maxine. Give him some rope. The man was probably nervous about being introduced to my best friend."

Months later, when Katie told Maxine she was going to marry Jeff and move to Rhode Island, Maxine had tried to talk her out of it.

"Why can't he move to San Francisco?" Maxine had asked.

"His job is back there," Katie answered.

"Yours is here. Your journalistic career is hot now. Think of the awards you've won for your investigative reporting. You'd have to start from scratch making new contacts. And you own a flat here," Maxine argued.

"I'll sell it. And Jeff is going to help me get additional funds to start my own women's periodical back east. You know I've had my heart set on that for a long time."

"So, what about those four kids of his?"

"His ex-wife has custody of the kids in Maryland."

"I don't know, Katie. He seems just too good to be true. And you're making all the sacrifices. I wish you wouldn't do this." Maxine paused and looked hard at Katie. "Not much chance of that, though, is there? Your eyes are gleaming like a damn homecoming queen. Just promise me, for God's sake, that you will at least cover your ass, Babe."

"I promise," Katie said.

Katie glanced up at the fluorescent lights again and whispered, "Sorry, old friend, I feel like I've broken that promise to you."

Jeff has let me down on every front, Katie admitted. And yet he is the one seething. She had smelled his anger in the car that very morning, strong and festering like sour milk.

In her rare moment of honesty, Katie accepted what she had probably known for months: There was only one way to satisfy Jeff, and that was to let him serve as czar over all their marital affairs, including *her* finances. She would have to use up all of her savings, quit her job to take care of his children full-time, have no source of income, have no joint accounts and trust him to do the right thing for her later, whenever that happened to be.

She pushed her tray to the other side of the table. That was it. She would have to put herself in his hands, body and soul, in order to pacify him. Her refusal to do this was causing him some kind of god-awful pain. His distress was real even if she believed his requests were unfair. If she refused to comply with his wishes, his anxiety would grow and one day he would pack up and leave her as he said he had his first wife. Although Katie couldn't make herself do what he wanted, thoughts of failing at her marriage were unbearable too. She conjured up an image whenever she pictured herself telling him to leave. *Jeff is walking slowly down the stone path, inside their dark hall she is pressing her face to the etched glass windows at the front door and watching him move further and further away into a dense fogginess, his figure is getting less distinct until it is no longer visible to her. Paralyzed at the window and alone, all she hears is the sound of her own breathing and heart pulsating against the old walls and tall slim windows.*

This miserable image and her awful admissions were unshakeable in her tonight. She didn't feel this way with his arms around her or when drowning in his violet blue eyes or holding hands in a movie or hunkered down for the night in their V-berth. Most of the time, she didn't let herself think this way. But this is how she was thinking this minute. She still loved him enough to break out in tears and feared she might soon produce a Niagara Falls in this booth. She picked up her napkin and twisted it between her fingers. Why couldn't she get him to meet her halfway? What was she doing that was so wrong? Why didn't he trust her; why did he need for her to take an oath of poverty in order for him to trust her? What was lacking in her that she couldn't get him to love her that much?

She ripped pieces off her napkin and set them side by side on the table. *Something is terribly wrong and I don't know how to fix it.* She had never let herself think this way before about anything. She picked up the strips of napkin and rolled them between her palms. *I'm failing. And I don't know what to do...I'm really failing.*

All her life she had believed there was a formula to solve each problem and that a person had only to concentrate hard enough and the right equation would reveal itself. The secret, she had always thought, *is in not giving up, in facing that screeching wind and darkening sky, riding the swells and cresting white caps, and when the storm has passed, being there to enjoy the slow breezes and stilled water and brilliant sunlight that will follow.* Yes, Katie knew how to survive and how to endure and how to succeed. But dear God, she realized now, she had never ever learned how to fail.

Katie bowed her head, elbows on the table in McDonald's. She recalled how optimistic she'd felt during their whirlwind courtship two years earlier in San Francisco and all those nightly long distance phone calls getting to know one another, sharing life's secrets, comparing beliefs, laughing at absolutely everything. And, of course, those romantic, monthly cross-country visits from Rhode Island that had swept her off her feet.

At twenty-seven, Katie had been something of an anomaly among her women friends in the 1970's world of new sexual freedoms. She had barely dipped a toe into those tantalizing waters. Instead, she had thrust all of her being into using her journalistic talents to advance social causes she believed in. Her friend Maxine had been as devoted as Katie in her support of anti-Vietnam war and feminist groups. And yet, Maxine never spent a Saturday night alone and almost never spent one with the same man twice.

Katie hadn't been desperate to have a permanent man in her life when she met Jeff O'Connell. She'd had her consciousness raised enough to understand she didn't need a lover in her bed to feel like a whole woman. Never mind the strength of her convictions, she'd plain and simple been smitten with Jeff, the sandy-haired, tall, broad shouldered, bright, ambitious Irish American who had wandered nonchalantly into her life.

She recalled how excited she'd been the morning a month after they met, carefully laying out her clothes on the bed – jeans, a bulky mohair sweater, rose-colored to complement her fair complexion, and black silk and lace underpants and bra. Imagining this would be the night she and Jeff would make love for the first time, she glanced self-consciously at her tall slender body in a full-length mirror when she stepped out of the shower. And felt a little more confidant as she dressed and tucked her long auburn hair behind her ears with tortoise shell combs.

Snatching up her packed overnight bag from the bed, she stopped in the living room and grabbed from the fireplace mantel her tiny porcelain elephant with one broken foot, the magic charm she'd found on the ground at a county fair in Minnesota when she was eleven. Back then it had fit perfectly in the pocket of her jeans. Now, whenever she was feeling tense and needing extra support, she tossed it in her bag where she could reach in and caress its soft satiny finish for reassurance. This was definitely one of those occasions, she decided on her drive to the airport.

Jeff held her hand while waiting at the rotating luggage terminal. "You're an elegant woman, even in jeans," he said. "Lovely as I remember." She smiled, feeling more secure with his large hand around hers.

When they were out of city traffic and had joined a stream of cars passing over the Golden Gate Bridge, he stretched out in the passenger seat. Having worked a full day before his five-hour flight, he closed his eyes and was asleep before they left the sun burnt hills of Marin County and headed north up the coastal highway. She glanced at him every so often, taking stock of him again, the light brown eyebrows, high cheekbones, his lips full and relaxed as he slept. He had unfastened the top button of his dress shirt and loosened his tie. She reached over and took his folded suit coat from his lap and tossed it onto the back seat, then waited until they were past Mendocino to touch his hand. "How about some last minute directions?" she asked him.

Rounding the last turn of a dirt road provided a first glimpse of Timberlane Inn, a stone and glass structure on a rocky cliff jutting out and overlooking the ocean. Surrounded on three sides by giant Sequoia, a four-foot high statue of Buddha stood guard at the center of a rock garden at the front entrance. In the main lodge, pine logs burned in a massive stone fireplace permeating the air with a smoky sweet aroma.

"I hadn't expected anything this inviting," she said while examining her surroundings. "How did you know about this place?"

"I spent a few weekends here after Charlene and I separated," he said. Katie's expression must have asked for further explanation. "By myself," he added. "I see it hasn't changed. I'm glad. Sometimes places disappoint you when you come back."

They registered at a desk under the eaves of a solid wood staircase and climbed the stairs to a loft area that circled the main lodge. Jeff went ahead of her, carrying one bag over each shoulder. She felt a trembling inside, excitement, not nerves, she was sure. The door opened into a bright, comfortable room, rough wood walls, thick quilts and down pillows on two attached beds. She walked over to a window that faced the courtyard with a view to the ocean and a calm came over her. Suddenly she felt perfectly at ease being alone with him in this room.

When she turned around, he was leaning against a far wall, watching her and smiling. He walked over and put his hand on her shoulder. "Don't be afraid – or uncomfortable. We're here to get better acquainted. That's all it has to be if you like."

"I haven't been with anyone – for a long while," she said. "My friend Maxine says I'm impossible to please. I can't explain even to myself why I'm here now. And I don't know why I'm telling you this." She glanced up at him. "And now I'm babbling, aren't I?"

He smiled. "I understand." He withdrew his hand from her shoulder. "We can go down to the lodge, have a drink and talk all night if you like."

"I'm fine. Really." *This will be all right*, she told herself.

The last of the daylight was dimming at the window. "If you're hungry we can have food brought to the room," he said. "I had dinner on the plane, but you're probably starved."

"Let's order something in a little while."

He touched her hair lightly at the side of her head. "Sandwiches maybe, or soup and an appetizer?"

"A shrimp cocktail will be perfect." She felt his fingers in her hair, the tip of one touching her ear.

I know so little about him...But I can do this. I want to do this...I will be all right. She took his hand from her hair and brought it to her lips. He held her at the waist with his other hand, close enough for her to feel the buttons on his shirt. She kicked off her shoes, and lifting herself, kissed his cheek lightly and then pulled back. Moving toward her again, he kissed her on the lips this time. They stayed with the kiss a long time until she drew away. Glancing first at his mouth, then into his eyes, she took his face in her hands and moved her fingers to his temples and through his sandy blond hair.

Slipping his hands under her sweater, he stroked her back, gently, then eased the sweater over her head and let it fall to the floor. She unbuttoned his shirt; he tossed it aside and brought her close to him again. Feeling the strength and tenderness of his touch she dropped her head to his chest and brushed her mouth over the fine hair. He moved her back from him, setting her into the corner of one arm while she unzipped her jeans, let them fall to her feet and kicked them away. Lowering her onto the bed, he eased her backward to a pillow, stood up and undressed, throwing the rest of his clothes over a chair. He sat next to her on the bed and removed her black lace bra and underpants, letting them fall to the floor. She felt as if she were in a dream without the power or desire to stop it; to stop it would surely defy everything that was natural.

One kiss blended into the next with the tips of tongues exploring inside. They stirred just enough for wet lips to brush against cheeks and temples, kissing throat and earlobes. His hands and mouth moved slowly over the slopes of her body, stopping where she guided him until she slid back to stroke him and caress him. Then he moved away from her, placing her head on the pillow again, and slipped his hands under her. Gathering him in, cradling him within her, she felt as though they'd known one another a very long time, had been together like this many times before.

Afterward he lay next to her with an arm around her shoulders. She slid one leg over him, burrowed her face into his chest and felt warm and insulated from the ocean wind rustling against their windows.

Tears had dampened her cheeks while reliving that magical night. She wiped them away with her wadded up napkin, got up, threw her trash into the bin and left the restaurant. How she hated to return to that dank old mausoleum. But, where else would she go? She could only hope that Jeff would have eaten something and fallen asleep watching television in their bedroom by the time she got home.

Chapter Three

Katie hesitated long enough on the stone path to glare at the gray shingled captain's house, its silhouette caught in a web of pine tree shadows, its slim windows like cat's eyes in the dark staring back at her. "I own you, you don't own me," she growled at the old cow of a mansion. She climbed the porch steps, opened the brass latch on the double front doors and went upstairs, but stopped short at their bedroom doorway. "Jeff, what do you think you're doing?" she gasped. "Why are you rifling through my bureau?"

"Searching for your phone book," he mumbled. "To call that bleeding heart reporter you hang out with to see if he might happen to know where you were. Tiny red veins speckled his cheeks; his forehead gleamed with perspiration. He slammed the drawer closed and stepped forward.

Katie moved away from the upward shove of his shoulders. Backing herself against a closet door, she said, "I was at McDonald's. I was only gone an hour."

He slapped his hand to the sliding door just above her shoulder.

Ducking under his arm and maneuvering around him she heard his heavy feet behind her as she made a dash for the staircase. Halfway down the stairs, she heard the thud of a shoe smacking hard against delicate banister poles. She let go of the railing, reeled around and stepped back from the sound of old mahogany cracking and the smell of wood being torn apart.

Now flattened against the opposite wall, she looked over her shoulder at Jeff whose knee was already bent and raised to land another blow sideways with the sole of his shoe. Paralyzed, Katie watched as one by one additional poles split open and splintered into haphazard ragged points that were no longer attached to the rail itself. Then the railing broke loose, toppled to one side and dangled at an angle toward the hallway below.

Her head whipped around in time to see Jeff retreating up the stairs and back into their bedroom. Then she swirled around and saw three children at the bottom of the stairs gaping up at her.

Heart pounding, she sank onto a step and held her head in her hands; the children were gone when she uncovered her eyes. Leaping up, she rushed to the den where thirteen-year-old Tommy had sprawled out on the floor in front of the television and older brother Mathew and eleven-year-old Martha huddled close to one another on the sofa. Katie lowered herself to a chair. "How are you guys doing?" She squeezed her hands together in her lap.

Tommy rolled over exposing his bare knees protruding from ripped jeans. He turned toward Katie. "Don't worry about the banister. He'll come home with whatever he needs to fix it tomorrow." He gave her one of his okay signs with his thumb and finger. "Just ride it out."

"Don't try to act so cool," Katie said. "I'm sure you're all as terrified as I am." She buried her head in her hands. "I can't cope with this. And you children shouldn't have to either."

"You look pale. You want a glass of water?" Mathew asked, his long legs stretched out in front of him on the carpet. Katie had almost forgotten how it felt to be sixteen years old. Ill at ease at best, she recalled, and this was far from best for this boy who'd been transported suddenly and permanently from one home to another. In spite of her own sense of crisis she had to fight an urge to walk over to him and put her arm around his shoulders. *But why at his age would he be trying to comfort me?*

"No, thank you. I just want to sit a minute," she said.

Mathew wiggled uncomfortably on the sofa and rubbed the insides of his sneakers together. "You're not going to pick up and leave, are you?" he asked.

"Leave?" Remembering that Mathew had been only eleven when his dad left his mother, Katie wondered how to answer him. "We're married, Mathew," she said finally, only Mathew's blank expression indicated that he needed more assurance than a marriage certificate.

Katie glanced away from Mathew to Martha. Martha's slim fingers fidgeted with the ends of curly blonde hair as she waited for Katie to continue. "I can't... we can't, live with this," Katie said, realizing at that very moment how much she had started to care about these kids. How could she leave them in this house? Jeff's tensions would multiply with the burden of handling everything himself. But she had no legal rights to take them with her. "I don't know," she said finally, the weight of her indefinite answer bearing down on her, her shoulders sagging with its possible implications.

Martha rose from the sofa. "I'm really tired. It's getting late." She stopped at the door and drew back her small shoulders. "Don't worry. Tommy's right. Everything will be fine by tomorrow or the next day. You'll see."

They all left the room but Katie stayed on in the den. She locked the door to the hall, took a coat of Jeff's from the closet and dragged it over to the sofa. What's wrong with these kids? They're acting like zombies when they ought to be hysterical.

If this were a nightmare, she would wake up in a cold sweat in the morning muttering thank God, none of this is real. But this would be much worse in daylight. Jeff had his boat; he had his private airplane; he had somehow grasped his children away from their mother. Yet she knew he had absolutely expressed anger at her with every muscle of his body tonight.

She grabbed at the coat yanking it tighter around her and then pulled her knees up fast to her stomach to try to control the shivering that had worked its way up from her feet to her neck. "This isn't happening to me. Men like this are with someone else. Not with me," she whispered into the collar of Jeff's coat.

In the past, she'd had a plan of action for the remote possibility that she would ever be confronted with such behavior. What had she sworn she would do? Leave him? Order him to leave? Easier, wasn't it, when the man seemed a faceless barbarian? Hugging her knees tighter to her middle, she rolled over, huddled closer to the sofa back and concentrated on sounds, old house timbers creaking, critters scrambling outside through the underbrush. With early morning grayish light already seeping between vertical slits in the window drapes, her eyelids finally grew heavy and she dozed off.

In the morning Katie heard Jeff leave earlier than usual and she called Mrs. Lewis with an excuse as to why she need not come to the house that day. Katie decided she and the kids would leave by the back door to avoid viewing the front hall wreckage again. Then she asked Mathew to take the earlier bus home from school with Tommy and Martha so they wouldn't be there alone.

So relieved to have made it through her workday, Katie had forgotten until she spotted the parked VW in their driveway that Jeff's oldest son Robert was coming home from college this weekend. Katie sighed. Facing that smug young man would be intolerable tonight. After observing the results of his dad's rampage, she knew handsome, cool Robert would place the blame on her. And he wouldn't have to say a word to do it. He would merely raise one eyebrow the way only he could to convey his thoughts – "so I see you've really provoked my father this time with your demands."

Robert let out a roar of laughter just as she opened the etched glass double doors into the hall where all four of Jeff's children had congregated. "Well, I guess Dad got some exercise last night," Robert said producing another burst of laughter.

Mathew whipped around to face Robert. "That isn't funny," he said, voice quivering, his face flushed. "Katie doesn't know how to deal with this stuff."

Katie swallowed hard because it was the first time she had heard one of them challenge Robert. In the next instant, Robert lunged at his brother, fastening a palm to each side of Mathew's head.

"Stop!" Katie screamed, but Robert had already backed Mathew into the wall and was holding him there. She tried to push herself between them. "Back away," she yelled at Robert but Robert shoved her aside and then started to pound Mathew's head against the solid oak paneling producing a sound like rock hitting pavement.

As blood spurted from the right side of Mathew's head and dripped into one of his eyes, Robert spat out the words, "Sissy bastard."

Finally letting go of Mathew's head, Robert gave Katie a scurrilous look. "Bitch," he growled as he sauntered down the hall.

"Quick, get into my car," Katie ordered Tommy and Martha who were clinging to one another in the corner of the hallway. "Mathew, stop by the kitchen sink. I'll get you ice and a towel to hold to your head. We're going to the emergency room."

Martha hid on the floor of the car in the parking lot, refusing to come into the clinic hospital with them. Thirty minutes later, a three-inch square of Mathew's scalp had been shaved, dressed and bandaged and X-rays of his head had been taken. "The wound will heal but he'll have a bad concussion," the doctor said as he wrote a prescription for pain and instructed Mathew to go to bed until his headache and dizziness were gone. Then he studied Mathew through his large horn-rimmed glasses and set a hand on his shoulder. "Tell your father to call me at once. Tonight! And tell him to speak to your brother immediately too. Do you understand? Go home and rest. I want to see you in two days."

"Okay," Mathew answered obediently.

"What did you tell the doctor?" Martha asked, still crouched on the floor between the seat and the dashboard when they returned to the car.

"Don't worry. Everything you tell doctors is confidential." Katie took in a deep breath. "Get in the back seat with Tommy, Martha. I want Mathew to sit up front."

Martha scanned the parking lot before moving and then got out and leapt into the back seat. "I'm not going back to school in Barrington Village if this gets out. I don't want everyone to know I'm from a weird family."

"Yeah, a second Addams Family," Tommy shrieked.

Martha covered her eyes with both hands. "Did we have to go to the hospital?"

Katie turned the ignition. "Look at your brother, Martha. Yes, we had to take him to the hospital." She glanced at Martha's scrunched-up face in the rear-view mirror. "I promise, doctors keep things to themselves."

Moving on nerves since morning, Katie gripped the steering wheel with both hands. She'd had to break up pushing and shoving skirmishes between the kids in the past, but nothing like this, nothing drawing blood, for God's sake. But how did she know what went on when she wasn't there? She thought about the times Robert had been alone with the rest of them, bruises from a baseball, falling from a tree, they had explained. Looking ahead at the black road, she envisioned the hall and, remembering last night's horror, felt clammy under her clothing. *Our Tower of London dungeon should be fumigated; we are all breathing contaminated air that is breeding a frightening disease.* For certain, she was going to call the nearest family services organization as soon as they got home.

"Well, if it isn't Florence Nightingale," Jeff said glaring at Katie as she and the kids trooped through the back door into the kitchen. He swung around in his chair at the table to get a better look at Mathew. "Look like Frankenstein's monster, buddy. Guess you'll live, though."

"This is serious," Katie said. "All of it. Last night and today." She glanced over at Robert who was leaning against the kitchen wall with his arms crossed and trying to mimic his father. She turned to Jeff. "I'm going to make an appointment for the kids and me with a family therapist and I want you to come along. I can't force you to come, but take a good look at that front hall and at Mathew's head before you decide."

Jeff swirled ice around in a glass and leaned back in his chair. "I'd like to know why you're making a federal case out of a couple of kids having a scuffle. Are you purposely trying to embarrass me in all of Rhode Island? I'm not speaking to the doctor or anybody else in this community about my family. Remember that. So don't have them call me."

Katie gestured toward Robert with her thumb. "He's not a kid anymore, Jeff. He's almost twenty years old. He can't go around beating up on people. What do you think this does to Mathew, in addition to his physical injury?"

"Maybe he should learn to fight back." Jeff picked out an ice cube from his glass and dropped it into his mouth.

Mathew stared in silence out the kitchen window. "Go lie down, Mathew," Katie said. "I'll come see you later." She focused on Jeff again. "I'm going to make the phone call to a social services organization this minute." She walked past everyone and down the hall toward the stairs.

Jeff's voice boomed out behind her. "The sky is falling. The sky is falling. If you want to piss and moan to someone, do it. But keep your hands off my kids. Don't you dare take my kids to some quack. I'm warning you!"

Chapter Four

Katie locked the bedroom door and called the State Public Health Department who referred her to Dr. Henry, a family therapist in Barrington. Hearing her frantic message on his voice mail, Dr. Henry answered immediately. "Come at once. I'll be waiting for you," he said, then gave her directions to his combined home and office south of the village.

Katie left the house quietly by the front door and twenty minutes later was ringing an office doorbell at the side entrance to a white-shingled Cape Cod style house. Dr. Henry, in a turtleneck shirt and a well-worn tweed jacket, swung open the door and reached for Katie's hand. "Come in, Mrs. O'Connell, follow me, please."

Except for a desk cluttered with file folders and a bookcase filled to capacity, the room felt more like a New England living room than an office. Katie sank gratefully into the overstuffed sofa the therapist offered her.

"Are the children safe now?" he asked her while seating himself in a brown leather chair facing her.

"They're okay," Katie said. "I'm glad you could see me tonight. It's short notice but I hope I can bring them to see you tomorrow."

"You can. But tell me how you're doing at the moment?"

"I'm exhausted but okay, I think."

"I have some fresh tea made. Can I bring you a cup?"

"That would be wonderful," she said realizing she hadn't had much to eat or drink all day.

Dr. Henry returned with a filled cup and a sugar bowl and creamer and set the tray on a table next to Katie. She took a few sips and then elaborated on what she had told him on the phone about the banister destruction and Robert's attack on Mathew. The therapist scribbled hurriedly on a lined pad to keep up with her rapid summing up of events and then put down his pen. "Now please tell me how the children came to live with you and Jeff."

"That remains a mystery to me," Katie said. "But I can tell you how I found out they were moving in with us."

"Yes, please."

"Jeff and I had only been married a couple of months when his ex-wife called him one night. This was about a year ago. I was in the kitchen when I heard him answer the phone. If I had picked up, there would have been a click followed by a dial tone. I know when it's her because a few minutes later she calls again and Jeff answers. I've never spoken to Charlene. 'You don't have to talk to her. I'll get information to you and Charlene if necessary,' is what Jeff told me from the beginning."

Dr. Henry ran his fingers through his mass of unruly gray hair, looked up and said, "Obviously he doesn't want you talking to one another." He picked up his pen and jotted down another note.

"To be truthful, Doctor, Jeff's attitude toward Charlene has created an aura of anonymity around the woman," Katie continued. "I've had to conjure up a whole person from a few snapshots, and from Jeff's original comments about her, and from some of the children's conversations I've overheard.

"In any case, from the kitchen that night I heard Jeff say, 'Good for you, Charlene. Wasn't I right about San Francisco?' At that, I stopped what I was doing and listened more carefully. A few minutes later Jeff strolled into the kitchen.

'Hi, Sweetheart,' he said. 'That was Charlene. She has sold the house in Maryland and moved out to San Francisco.'

"'She what? Why San Francisco?' I blurted out. I was really confused because Jeff had just picked up the kids in his private plane the day before to spend the weekend with us. 'When did Charlene leave Baltimore?' I asked Jeff.

"'I put her on a United plane yesterday afternoon and then flew back to Rhode Island with the kids,' Jeff said."

"Are you saying the kids were already at your home when she called?" Dr. Henry asked Katie.

"Oh, yes. They were there all right. I was shocked, Doctor, but as his news started to sink in it started to dawn on me that maybe this could be a good thing. With Charlene and the kids in California, Jeff and I could at last be newlyweds and the kids could visit us during vacations and summers as we had planned before we were married.

"The next thing Jeff said was, 'I found her a nice apartment when I was in San Francisco last week.'

"I shook my head in disbelief at that, but my mind shifted quickly back to the kids. 'Are you sure an apartment will have enough room for the children?' I asked him.

"'The kids are staying back east,' he said, just like that, matter of fact."

"'Where?' I sputtered.

"'With us, of course,' he said.

"'Do the children know?' I asked him because nothing would have surprised me right about then.

"'Of course,' Jeff said.

"And then I hollered at him, 'For God's sake! And none of you thought to ask my opinion!' I fell back against the nearest wall and started to bawl hysterically.

"'Charlene has had them for four years,' he said. 'Now it's my turn. She's earned this opportunity.'"

"'What opportunity?' I blurted out.

"'A lot has changed. I have a wife now, don't I? And this great big house,' he said.

"'Aren't you the fuckin' lucky one, Jeff?' is all I could think to say.

"'I didn't expect you to react this way,' Jeff said, frowning as if I'd disappointed him something terrible.

"'You didn't think about me one way or the other,' I told him."

Dr. Henry shook his head. "And how did you feel that moment?"

Katie tossed her head back. "Used – hired help who didn't need to be consulted."

"How else *could* you have felt? So, what did you do next? What did you say to the kids?" Dr. Henry asked.

Katie took up where she'd left off. "An hour after the phone call we all sat down to the dinner I'd cooked when thinking the kids would be with us for three days, not eternity. Jeff watched me moving around, placing a bowl of mashed potatoes and a platter of chicken on the table. His eyes caught mine as I settled into my chair at the other end of the table and then his lips actually formed the words 'I love you'.

"Martha, Mathew and Tommy slid into their chairs. Jeff was radiant, little flecks of light illuminating his eyes. He sat poised at his end of the dining table, looking satisfied with his children lined up on each side. Martha was trying to act self-assured; Tommy slouched in his chair waiting for dinner to be done with. Then I noticed that Mathew, always trying to please, had showered and changed into a clean shirt and jeans for dinner and had combed his damp short hair slickly behind his ears. Attractive glib college boy Robert took over the conversation interrupting the others and laughing hardest at his father's jokes."

"I'm sure you were seething by then," Dr. Henry said. He stopped to write an additional notation on his pad and then looked long and hard at Katie. "I don't know how you got through that meal."

"Neither do I, Doctor."

"I can assure you my anger had been building since the phone call. Just a few minutes before everyone sat down at the table, I'd been seized by an urge to flee from the house through the back door with my car keys in my hand. I had to hold onto the kitchen counter to stop myself. I knew the kids were hungry so I just started to serve the food.

"At one point, I remember, while sitting at the table, I turned to Tommy and asked him what I knew would be an incredible question: 'Have any of you talked to your mother since she arrived in San Francisco yesterday?'

"You see, Doctor, Jeff has this way of separating people from one another. It's as if he locks them up in individual containers and shoves the keys into his own pocket. So I wasn't surprised that my question hovered unattended somewhere above the chicken platter and the salad bowl. The table went cold silent; Martha and Mathew stopped eating. I could feel the cut of Jeff's glare without even looking at him. I could imagine his eyebrows raised and his lips clamped shut. I'd opened his strong box stamped 'original O'Connell family'. The perfect family that had come apart at its seams is how I thought of them.

"I might as well have asked Tommy how many girls he'd molested on his school bus during the past year as to inquire about their mother.

"Anyway, I got no answer from the kids because Robert decided to change the subject immediately. Suddenly clapping his hands above his head, he said, 'Let's vote on something fun to do next weekend.'

"How I wished I'd been able to read the three younger kids' minds that minute. How must they have felt about their mother moving three thousand miles away? Possibly the same as I had, I figured – that some kind of dirty trick had been played on all of us.

"There was a moment when all of their voices started to mesh growing more and more faint until I could barely hear them at all. At the same time I began to feel weightless and then free floating and the next thing I felt myself spiraling upward through a bright tunnel of light to a wide-open space beyond. From below, I watched myself traveling further and further away, becoming a tiny speck, and finally disappearing entirely. Although physically remaining at the table I became merely an observer from that point on. The next morning, however, reality slapped me in the face. There were still four additional people living with us."

Pulling herself up on the sofa, Katie said, "I apologize, Dr. Henry. I suppose I'm telling you more than you need to know, but it's so good to unload. I haven't had anyone to talk to."

"I'm glad you feel you can do that here. Besides, I have to know as much as possible if I'm going to try to help you and the children. In fact, I have another question for you. Do you know why Charlene was willing to give up her children? It's hard to understand, don't you think?"

"I can't fathom it either. All Jeff told me was that she wanted to finish her BA degree and needed the time and space to do it."

"Has Jeff told you much about that first marriage?"

"His only reflective comment to me about their marriage occurred on our very first date. He was looking at my diploma from the University of California that I had framed and placed on my fireplace mantel and said, more or less in these words: 'I wish Charlene had been as ambitious as you. Having four babies in seven years seemed to overwhelm her. Our home was always in chaos. I buried myself in our bedroom evenings to escape the confusion. After a while, she let herself go personally. She didn't seem interested in anything. Finally, one night I packed a suitcase and left and didn't go back.'

"I was shocked at his abrupt ending at the time and I've wished ever since that I'd said something to defend the poor woman. She must have been devastated when he walked out on her like that. After Jeff had revealed that much to me, he seemed too distressed to continue the subject. I tried to find out more about Charlene later but he has told me nothing else. I should have tried to find out more. I wish now I'd been smart enough to do that."

Dr. Henry stood up, came over and touched her on the shoulder. "You and those kids need support now. Can you all be here at noon tomorrow?"

"Oh, yes. It's a Saturday. I'll beg them to come with me and promise them pizza afterward. Even if I invited Robert he wouldn't join us but I think the others will."

* * * * * * *

The seriousness of having defied Jeff weighed heavily on Katie as soon as she and the children were seated in Dr. Henry's office. With his bushy gray eyebrows knotted, Dr. Henry surveyed their group: Martha and Mathew squeezed together on a small sofa, Tommy's body slouched and sunken into the shape of his large plump chair, and Katie squeezing her hands together nervously in her lap and hoping for a miracle.

Circling the room, Dr. Henry elicited a name from each of the kids and then asked them their ages.

Tommy, chin resting on his chest, mumbled, "Thirteen plus" into his T-shirt.

"Eleven years, two months," Martha said locking eyes with the therapist.

"Sixteen," said Mathew, a bandage still clinging to the side of his head.

"We have a problem," Katie said, stating what the therapist could see for himself.

Dr. Henry scribbled furiously again onto his yellow pad as the children answered his individual questions about their schools and friends. Then he sat back and appraised everyone again. "Katie has told me you've had a rough time at home the past couple of days. Who wants to tell me more about what happened?" He peered at them through thick horn-rimmed glasses, and getting no volunteers, turned back to Katie. "How often does this kind of violence occur in your home?" he asked her.

"Violence?" she stuttered. She was going to follow up by saying, "But he's never touched me," but noting Dr. Henry's incredulous expression, she went silent.

Then Tommy filled the sudden void in conversation. Speaking in an emotionless voice that shook Katie by the shoulders, he said, "My brother Robert has been busting on me and Mathew since I was about five years old."

"And your father?" Dr. Henry asked.

Tommy shrugged, "Oh, him, he's always taken mentals."

Inspecting the group once more, Dr. Henry asked anyone who would answer, "What would you do when your father took these mentals?"

"We would lay low," Mathew offered. "My mother always told us to become invisible and speechless the second he started in."

His mother always told them? Mathew's calm answer confirmed Katie's worst suppositions, ending any lingering doubts about their past.

Martha, pressing a palm to her forehead, closed her eyes. "Will this conversation stay secret? Because I don't want to be any part of it. I'm only here as a favor to Katie."

"Yes, this is confidential, but do you mind talking about your family?" Dr. Henry asked.

"I'm not talking. Katie is, and them." She crooked her thumb at Tommy and Mathew. "I don't like people badmouthing my father. He's perfectly fine, except when..." She lifted the curly blonde hair at the back of her neck and let it fall back onto her shoulders. "My father is president of the Rhode Island branch of International Computer." She narrowed her eyes at Dr. Henry. "I wasn't sure you knew that."

"I know that. I've read about him. Only we do have to talk about his temper if it's hurting his family. We're not saying he's a bad person."

Martha frowned. "I don't know if I'm coming back then."

The therapist turned to Tommy and Mathew. "How about you two? Are you up for another meeting?"

Tommy hunched up his shoulders and replied, "I guess."

"I'm coming," Mathew answered.

"And you?" he asked Martha.

She produced a long sigh. "I'll think about it."

"How about 4:30 on Tuesday then? We can discuss anything at all you want to next time. We had a good start today."

Dr. Henry glanced over at Martha. "I'm looking forward to seeing all of you in a few days then."

He turned back to Katie and offered her his professional card. "My twenty-four-hour number. Call me if there's an emergency before then."

Katie waited for a riot to break out when everyone was safely back in her car but instead their chatter turned to a critique of a new *Star Wars* movie. Evidently Dr. Henry had passed muster with them. But then, when had she ever seen these kids protest anything outright? Katie sighed and questioned whether there was even the remotest chance that their emotions, seemingly anaesthetized for so long, could be resuscitated by Dr. Henry.

Chapter Five

The following night, three days after Jeff had kicked the banister off its poles, a Chamber of Commerce dinner had been scheduled to name Jeff Rhode Island Man of the Year. With communication between Jeff and Katie non-existent and Katie sleeping in the den, they hadn't yet discussed the horrific events of the past week. Katie's brain had felt too numb to make plans beyond taking the kids to their next appointment with Dr. Henry. Last night, she'd left a note on Jeff's bureau giving him the name of an AMA psychiatrist, and this morning found it torn to shreds in a wastebasket.

They would have to speak sooner or later, but what was there to say? Thinking about the dinner that evening was giving her a headache. If she didn't show up, she knew there would be consequences: the children's friends would ask why she wasn't standing by Jeff's side in tomorrow's front page picture; she would have to explain her peculiar absence from the award ceremony to Natalie, her editor in chief, and to the photographer who would be covering the event. And what could she possibly tell them? Popping two Tylenols into her mouth, Katie washed them down with a swallow of coffee and tossed the container back into her desk drawer. Oh, hell, it might be easier to attend the damn affair and play the role of devoted wife for a few hours than have to lie to people, she decided.

* * * * * * *

Cameras flashed as Katie and Jeff climbed seemingly endless stairs leading up to the entrance of the gray shingled historic Barrington Yacht Club. A few weeks ago she had actually looked forward to this night and to wearing the white silk jacket and long black skirt she'd bought for the occasion. Jeff, his hand cupped under her elbow, escorted her inside to the formal dining area where the International Computer management and invited guests awaited him. His blue eyes electric, smile dazzling, he made his way through the crowd greeting people while clamping an arm on shoulders all along the way.

Lifting two champagne glasses from a tray, he gave one to Katie, and, slipping a hand around her waist, smiled obligingly for Hank, the *Gazette* photographer. Then he bent down and whispered to Natalie at the nearby press table. "How are you tonight, Natalie?"

"Doing nicely," Natalie said, parting her lips to smile in a way that startled Katie at first, then amused her. Jeff wandered off and Natalie, looking confident and lovely as ever in a green velvet gown that complemented her tawny complexion and black hair, suddenly became flustered. She nudged Katie. "My, what an attractive man he is." She laughed with a shake of her shoulders, "For him, I might have left San Francisco, too."

Viewing Jeff through the eyes of Natalie and the assembled guests, Katie saw a fine figure of a man and a charismatic talented leader. But she had a simultaneous thought as well. None of these people would believe her; they would never accept her word over his about anything. And then she wondered why she was even entertaining this notion.

Representative Ronald Wilson, their steely-eyed district congressman, sat next to her at the long VIP table at the front of the dining hall. Brandishing a wide grin, he gushed, "So glad to meet Jeff O'Connell's pretty wife." Katie stiffened for an evening even worse than the one she had anticipated. She disagreed with everything this right wing congressman stood for.

"Katie O'Connell," she answered to specify that she had a name of her own.

"Well, Katie," he said, seeming pleased to be making use of her first name. "I understand why Jeff is so successful. How could he go wrong with such a charming wife at home?"

"I'm a staff writer at the *Gazette*."

"Well, I'm sure you're proud of your husband tonight."

She nodded. Of course she was proud of Jeff's accomplishments so why did she have to squelch an urge to flutter her eyelashes at her dinner mate and respond, "Yes, I was proud of him until last Friday when he kicked the banister off our foyer staircase." The very next second, she envisioned herself leaping up from her chair, facing the entire room and screaming: "None of you really knows this man I am living with!"

Forty-five minutes later, Katie, grateful to have made it to dessert and coffee, prayed that the speeches would be short as Al Demings, president of the local Chamber of Commerce, stood up and started to introduce Jeff. "Through expansion of International Computer in Rhode Island, Jeff O'Connell has created five hundred additional jobs in the coastal area," he said, then turned to Jeff seated at his right. "But I'll let him explain these miracles for himself. We are proud to present our Man of the Year award. Let's give him a hand, everyone."

On his way to the microphone Jeff placed his hand gently on Katie's shoulder. His speech, moving and humorous, was interrupted often by applause. Then suddenly at the end, he swept a hand through the air in Katie's direction. "Let me finish by saying I couldn't have managed any of this without my wife Katie. She holds the fort, making sure there's milk in the fridge, getting kids to their appointments and checking on homework while I'm cruising the country in search of new business opportunities. 'They also serve who wait' or however that goes. Without Katie, I'd be the one staying home doing the laundry." Laughter rippled through the room as Jeff swished his hand toward Katie again.

Katie darted a quick glance over at the press table. Natalie was busy taking notes. Perhaps she'd been too distracted to hear Jeff's praise of the "little woman", Katie hoped. She supposed she ought to enjoy any appreciation from Jeff, but instead, she felt as if she'd been zipped into a dress two sizes too small. Who was this woman, anyway, that Jeff had just described? Had she sprung from the whole cloth of his imagination, or, God forbid, had she become her when she wasn't looking? He could have mentioned her work at the *Gazette*. Or, both would have been nice. She took a drink of ice water. Why dissect his words, choking the life out of what may have been an actual expression of gratitude? *Oh, sure, it was. After scaring the hell out of me only three days ago?*

Back from the microphone, Jeff lifted Katie's hand. "I hear the band starting up," he said. "Would you like to dance?"

He led her onto the dance floor and, holding her closely at the waist, smiled down at her and said, "I hope you're enjoying yourself."

"Fine affair. You've worked hard and you deserve the award," she answered honestly.

"Thank you," he said setting his cheek against hers. "Let's leave in about ten minutes."

Other couples had begun to fill the dance floor. "It's only ten o'clock," she said. "Will it be protocol for you to leave so soon?"

"I'm their honored guest." He smiled at acquaintances on the dance floor while responding, "I can depart when I please."

Katie had gotten used to Jeff giving her time limits, but the last few days had been a strain, and now that the formalities were over, she felt like enjoying the music for a while. Or, was it really because she wasn't anxious to go home? Over Jeff's shoulder, she spotted Jeff's chief marketing man, stockily built, red-faced Jack Flynn who was flapping his arms and motioning for them to join his table.

Giving Katie a bear hug, Jack said, "Jeff, mind if I borrow your wife for a dance?"

Jeff checked his watch. "Okay, but we're leaving in a few minutes. I'll round up the car and meet you outside," he told Katie while still clasping Jack's hand. "Enjoy the rest of the evening," he told everyone at Jack's table. Katie watched him heading toward the front exit while accepting more congratulations along the way.

"If you want to stay longer, Doris and I can give you a ride home," Jack said while guiding Katie onto the floor.

She glanced at her own watch, gauging that it would take the attendant a few extra minutes to locate their car in the crowded parking lot. "Well, you know Jeff when he decides to do something," she offered.

"I feel for you," Jack said. "I'm sure what we see is only the tip of the iceberg."

Taken aback, Katie wasn't sure she'd heard him correctly. She decided to gamble. "Jeff's under a lot of stress lately. I'm trying to persuade him to get some counseling." She paused, and then ploughed on ahead. "I wonder if you could have a talk with him, Jack? He respects you so much."

Jack hesitated forever it seemed to Katie before answering. "I think he would resent my interference," he said finally. "I'd like to help but...I hope you understand, Katie."

"Of course," she said, horrified that she had asked Jack to do such a thing, and wishing she could take it back. Had she expected him to say, "Of course, Katie, tomorrow I'll stroll into my boss's office and tell him to get his act together"? That was stupid of her, jumping on his remark like that, probably an innocent comment. "Tip of the iceberg," he could have meant anything. But when she looked into Jack's eyes again she knew that her first impression had been right. His smile was apologetic, yet helpless, and Katie felt sorry for him.

Jack's petite, good-natured wife Doris had returned to their table by the time the dance ended. "Give my congratulations to your husband," she said. "I don't see him this minute."

"I will but he's already left and waiting in the car. I suppose I'd better join him. Have fun, all. See you soon, everyone."

She and Jeff returned to their previous silence in the car on the way home. She understood why these bright and beautiful people admired Jeff. He was everything that the award speeches said he was – energetic, enterprising, creative. But he also had another side. He had a terrible temper; she and the kids could attest to that. Unfortunately, she seemed to be the only one making it a problem. The children, to their own detriment, Katie believed, had learned to cope with his erratic behavior. Jeff had already gotten someone to repair the banister and would as soon forget the awful incident had ever occurred. Without her stubbornness, in fact, everyone could pick up where they had left off a few days ago. She had definitely been cast as the family troublemaker. At least she was getting the kids the therapy they needed. Would it hurt to ease up a little? My God, she was sick of being the family drudge and ever-present reminder of gloom and doom.

Jeff went straight to bed when they got home and was already asleep when Katie came upstairs to get a nightgown from her bureau drawer. She folded her arms and watched him lying there quiet and peaceful in their bed for a few seconds and then went into the bathroom to change. On her way back from the bathroom she stopped alongside their bed, listened to his quiet breathing and then shivered thinking how she would feel sleeping all alone in the den. She went around to the other side of the bed, and without planning to or meaning to, lifted a corner of the quilt and crawled between the bedclothes.

Sometime during the night Jeff stretched an arm and a leg over her and curled up to her back. In the morning, she heard him singing in the shower. "Morning, Katie," he said, coming out of the bathroom with a towel around his waist and looking eager to start his day.

A sense of dread washed over Katie. *And of shame, too, for having surrendered to a moment of panic, giving him the impression that all was well.*

A month later, at one of their secret sessions with Dr. Henry, Katie broke down for the first time. Sobbing, she blubbered, "I'm battling fear every day. I don't want Jeff to find out about the therapy. I don't like having to do this without him. I don't like asking the kids to keep something from him. I don't know what's going to happen next."

Tommy bobbed up, grabbed a handful of Kleenex from a box on the table next to him and brought it to her. She blew her nose. "I don't honestly know how to help any of us."

"He's not going to change," Mathew said, his voice cracking midstream the way it did whenever he tried to voice an opinion. "As for me, I have plans. I'm going to keep smiling until I'm out of the house and away at college."

Tommy snickered. "One time my dad ran over my tricycle purposely 'cos it was in the driveway. He had reversed to get speed up first. I ran away and hid in a field for two hours. When I came back, he acted like nothing happened. So I did too. Just as if nothing had happened. That's what works for him."

Martha, who had slowly begun to participate in their discussions, shook her head and rolled her eyes. "Any one of us could tell better stories than that, Tommy."

"What's really important," Dr. Henry said, "is how you feel about the stories and about your father and about yourselves."

"I'm okay," Martha said. "I love my father, but I wish he'd stop throwing fits. I get scared when he does and I'm always waiting for the next one to happen. I hate that about me. I wish I could stop that."

Tommy slumped further into his chair and studied his scuffed and dirty sneakers; his stringy shoulder length hair fell forward hiding much of his perfect face. "I'd get mad at him, but what good would it do? He made my mother cry and now Katie's crying."

Mathew thumped his fingers on a side table. "I hate when he goes nuts, and then I feel sorry for him and hate myself for not staying mad at him. Oh, boy. He would hate to hear me say I feel sorry for him. He would really hate that."

Half an hour later, Dr. Henry pushed back his chair and stood up. "Good work today," he said. "I'll see you all in a week."

"Want to try that brand new Mexican restaurant in the village?" Katie asked as they all filed out of Dr. Henry's cottage. "You know Mrs. Lewis isn't expecting you for dinner tonight."

"Si, Señora." Tommy twisted an imaginary moustache. "Si, si. I'm starving."

"I love tacos." Martha either loved or hated things this month. She scooted closer to Katie and away from the boys as they walked, and then smoothed her sweater at her slim hips. "Half my middle school will be there and look what I wore today."

"That sweater matches your sky blue eyes," Katie assured her.

"Could we sit at a different table from them?" She notched her head toward Mathew and Tommy who straggled behind them.

"They'll behave," Katie said, although she was never absolutely sure about Tommy.

"Order anything. I feel rich today," Katie said, as they slid into a round corner booth at The Chilli Pepper. Martha quickly scanned the room.

"Anybody important here, Martha?" Katie asked her.

"Only one," she whispered, a hand covering her lips. "The rest are all creeps."

"Which one is important?" Katie couldn't have guessed without help.

"Over there." Martha rolled her eyes in the direction of a boy with a mop of brown curly hair. He waved from his table and Martha flicked her hand slightly from the wrist, then opened her menu and hid behind it. "He's so wicked gorgeous, I'm sure he's conceited," she whispered to Katie.

Katie smiled; she'd forgotten the dance, but the steps were coming back. "Okay, let's get serious everybody. We have to go up to the counter to order." Tommy came back with a tray and ate half of his super combo plate before speaking again.

"I was wondering if I could have some kids over one of these Friday nights," he said.

Katie sprinkled oil and vinegar on her salad. "If we're talking about a party, you'll have to ask your dad."

"Maybe we can have it when he's away on business," Tommy said, then wiped his mouth with a napkin. "I've given this a lot of thought. Music and chow."

"Pretty deep thinking, Tommy," Martha said, taking a dainty mouthful of her taco.

Suddenly producing one of his light-up-the-room smiles, Tommy sputtered, "Big problem. Figuring out which girls to invite 'Cos they all love me so."

"No pot. No beer. Understand?" Katie told him

"You can trust him," Mathew said. "He's a flake, but he won't screw you on this."

"Tell you what, Mathew," Katie said. "I'll put you in charge that night."

"Yuk," Tommy said, throwing his head back against the seat.

"Martha, you're head of decorations."

"On one condition," Martha said pointing to Tommy. "His grubby friends have to promise not to attack my work."

"I'm insulted!" Tommy gasped. "And insulted double for my friends."

Katie looked fondly around the table at each of them remembering the day she had first met them all. Standing a few feet back from Jeff's car in their driveway, she had watched them pile out, one by one.

Mathew, fifteen, wearing clean jeans and a windbreaker zipped up to his neck, appeared first. "Pleased to meet you," he said, offering her his hand.

Next, Tommy, ripped jeans, stringy blond hair to his shoulders, leaped from the back seat and yelled, "Yo...me too."

Then ten-year-old Martha climbed out of the back seat. Pushing back frizzy blonde bangs from her eyes, she looked up at Katie. "Hello, I'm Martha," she said. Ducking around to the trunk, she took an overnight bag from her oldest brother, Robert.

Robert, a tall, handsome nineteen-year-old, closed the trunk lid, and then took his time examining Katie before giving her a curt hello.

Katie glanced around the restaurant and back at the kids again. "A party could be fun, guys," she said realizing that they *almost* sounded like a normal family. And that she *nearly* felt like a mother treating her kids to a dinner out. Who would guess? Only she and the kids knew better, much better.

Chapter Six

Jeff had been walking around with a self-satisfied look about him ever since the night of the Chamber of Commerce dinner, which surprised Katie because she had gone back to sleeping in the den the following night. It had been three weeks since Jeff had wreaked havoc in the front hall and Robert had attacked Mathew and nothing whatsoever had been resolved. Jeff would never mention the incident himself and Katie hadn't whipped up enough energy to hash it out with him. Perhaps this was why he was smiling. And now another emergency could not be ignored. She had already used half of the proceeds she'd earned from the sale of her condo in San Francisco. And now, besides her personal and household expenses she was paying for the children's therapy as well.

She simply had to force Jeff to face these realities. She had come home from work early, seeped a pot of tea and sent the kids to their wing of the house so she and Jeff could talk privately.

"Sit down, Jeff," she said as soon as he opened the back door. "We must have a discussion." She poured tea into two cups. "This is urgent so please listen." She had to speak quickly before he had a chance to blow up. "You must deposit some money into my checking account."

He remained standing. "Later," he said. "I sense you're about to become emotional again. That job is running you ragged. I want you to quit working. Damn, Katie, I have financial plans in place for us."

She slapped the palm of her hand to her forehead. "To go into effect when? I'm almost broke, Jeff. You can't have a wife serving all your needs and refuse to pay her bills. And then expect her to take care of you and your children until she's penniless. That's friggin' crazy! What woman would agree to that? I gave up my job and my home and my friends and all my security to move across the country!" She took in a quick breath. "Put some money in my account now!" She rubbed her hands together on the table. "This is not up for discussion. You have to meet me at the bank at noontime tomorrow."

With his face reddening and eyes narrowing, Jeff walked over to the sink and gazed out the window. Wishing he were out there with those sickly pine trees, anywhere but here, Katie supposed.

Then he swung around, grabbed up his briefcase from the table smacking it hard against the refrigerator on his way out of the kitchen.

Katie stared numbly after him a few seconds realizing that his sudden angry actions no longer shocked her as they used to. Instead she guessed at the logic or illogic of Jeff's thinking. *Today I feel as though I've been sucked back in time to Ibsen's Doll's House,* she thought. *Am I supposed to contribute my efforts and money without hurting his pride by mentioning the fact?*

She got up, grabbed a skillet from a cabinet, plucked a package of beef patties from the refrigerator and slapped them into a frying pan on the hot stove. A vision of her neat, peaceful Pacific Heights flat, the ornamental plaster work on the ceiling, the wide bay windows, the marble fireplace, flashed before her as she glanced out the kitchen window at the puny pine trees out back. How she longed for the sight of a sturdy old dependable Redwood. She backed away and walked down the hall to the children's wing. "How about straightening up this room, kids? It's pretty frightful. Hang up your jackets. Pick up the wet towel on the chair. Your books belong on the desk," she wondered why she was always the one passing out instructions when suddenly her question was interrupted by a whiff of smoke drifting down the hall from the kitchen.

By the time she reached the stove, red and blue flames were leaping into its hood. Pushing things aside in a cabinet, she grabbed a box of baking soda and shook it over the smoldering hamburgers that were already forging to the skillet. She reached for a potholder, brought the pan to the sink and held it under the cold water faucet. Steam, hissing and spitting, rose up wetting her face and stinging her eyes. She dropped the frying pan into the sink and yanked open the kitchen window.

Damn, she'd let the aborted discussion with Jeff distract her. Good thing these priceless 1850 wooden cabinets weren't damaged; the historic society might have had her flogged in the village square. Bad enough, some of them were streaked with gray smoke stains and would have to be scrubbed tomorrow.

"Shit," she muttered, swinging open the refrigerator door. Scanning quickly, she reached into the freezer and pulled out a package of franks.

When she turned around, Jeff was behind her, eyebrows scrunched together. "Can't you cook some damn hamburgers without burning them?"

"What? The nerve! And why by the way am I making dinner?" she asked him. "We were going to take turns cooking for you and me when Mrs. Lewis started making dinner for the kids. Guess you forgot that?"

He turned around making another swift exit, sweatshirt and jogging pants flapping down the hall. She heard his feet stomping on the stairs, then the bedroom door smacking shut. She sucked in a breath. "What the hell?" she stammered.

Three kids, Tommy, Mathew and Martha, wide-eyed, mouths open, rushed into the kitchen as soon as their father was out of sight. "Danger's over, guys," Katie said. But never fear. Wonder Woman came to the rescue. Probably saved all our lives."

Martha giggled, nodding agreement. Tommy looked disappointed that the excitement was cut short.

Katie threw an arm around Tommy's shoulder. "Good thing the three of you already had your dinner. Count your blessings. Everybody go back to the wing now and do your homework."

An hour later she gazed out the kitchen window again. The spindly pine trees were now making spider shadows against the moon. She backed away; they were getting closer, no question about it.

I wanted to love Jeff forever but why is he plowing through our rose garden with a John Deer tractor? Katie wondered. She had stopped herself from chasing him up the stairs to demand that he talk to her. Apologize is what she meant. Now, hours later, she climbed the stairs gingerly and foolishly, she supposed, to repeat her request for funds.

He was pulling off a sweatshirt and getting ready for bed when she got to the bedroom. "I expected you to come downstairs to say you were sorry for insulting me," she said.

He glanced at her over his shoulder. "Okay. I apologize. It was great to start a fire."

"Funny, Jeff. What was I supposed to tell the kids when you stayed upstairs all evening?"

He took off his sweatpants, folded them carefully and set them on a closet shelf. "They understand, I'm sure."

His smug expression infuriated her. "Understand you get furious and disappear when there's a problem, you mean?"

He yanked a clean T-shirt over his head. "Damn, Katie. With three or four kids around, you have to pay attention. You have to anticipate trouble every minute." He slapped a flat hand onto the closet door. "How can you keep track of things when you're gone all day?"

"Number one, it's not up to *me* to keep track of everything. And second, I wouldn't sit around anticipating trouble if I *were* here all day. She ran her fingers through her hair, looping a handful behind one ear. "You wanted to have your children with you. You have to be a real parent now. And that involves more than entertaining them on weekends. Even with Mrs. Lewis overseeing them for a few hours in the afternoon they create a lot of work every day and on weekends."

Katie left the bedroom and went back downstairs to the wing to make sure the kids had gone to their rooms. Then she went to the den and flipped on the television to a channel where David Brinkley was issuing his latest Watergate bulletin. How she and her old friend Maxine would have relished seeing Nixon squirm, finally getting his due, but Katie felt unconnected to that world lately, her thoughts slipping easily away from Nixon's transgressions back to Jeff's change of personality. Shutting off the TV, she wandered down the hall to their dark living room and flopped into a lounge chair.

If Jeff had wanted his kids so badly, why hadn't he planned for their daily care? This struck Katie as out of character for an organizer like Jeff, but then she snickered to herself and sighed with her whole body. *Of course, I nearly forgot – he had expected to have live-in help.* Naturally, she and Jeff wouldn't have continued trying to please each other every minute, loving everything about the other person. But how could she have imagined that their lives would have changed so abruptly after marriage?

He brought his kids here without a thought to what it took to keep a home in operation – all the lugging and scrubbing and marketing and cooking, any more than her own father had paid any attention to such things, Katie recalled. And now Jeff's face lights up, just as her father's had, when he had his wife at one end of the table and his children lined up on either side of him. Jeff's violet eyes fairly dance, lips curving into captivating grins, when he is pleased with his kids, a good meal, their love making. *My mother had provided my father with these pleasures but in turn he had taken care of her needs,* Katie remembered. Yet Jeff expects to receive the first half of that bargain without fulfilling the second.

Only a year and a half ago, she wouldn't have believed that she and Jeff would ever be fussing over house and kids and money issues. The idea would have seemed preposterous. Back then, Jeff was squiring her around on his arm, wining and dining her; nothing had been too much trouble if it made her smile. *Now he is reluctant to open a damn joint bank account with me.*

Katie folded herself more comfortably into a soft leather lounge chair and dozed off until a shuffling noise in the hall woke her. Startled, she sat up, her head swirling around as a form materialized from the dark hall, then appeared in the archway. In the next moment, an object, a glass, she noted somewhere in the back of her mind, hurtled through the air. Passing barely above her head, it crashed against the opposite wall, points of light glittering and forming arcs in front of one of the tall windows.

The form moved from the archway into the living room, moonlight seeping through the windows giving it shape as it lurched forward.

"Jeff," she screamed with an unrecognizable sound that must have come all the way from her gut. She rose up from her chair, legs moving of their own accord it would seem, and ran through the archway into the hall. She heard him behind her, his feet moving faster than hers until suddenly they stopped short. She reeled around in time to see his knuckled fist smash like the single burst of a jackhammer into the living room wall. Hunks of plaster jettisoned from the edges of his fist, dust particles descending to the floor. Eyes flashing, he spun around.

She leaped backwards out of his way as he darted from the room, each of his feet slamming solidly down on the wooden floor in the hall and then on up the stairs. The bedroom door banged shut. Katie gasped, clutching her arms to her chest, and hugging herself, slowly taking in air until she felt she could walk. Nerves moving muscles, she sprang forward, grabbing her purse from a telephone stand. On her way to the front door she heard sounds coming from the other wing. God, the kids, she remembered, racing over to them and stopping at the foot of their staircase.

Martha was crouched on the top step, her fingers twisting a satin ribbon at the neck of her pink flannel nightgown. "I heard you yell," she said in a thin little voice. "It's okay. My dad will be fine now. I promise you. He's back up in his bedroom, isn't he?"

"Yes," Katie said. "Are you all right?"

Martha nodded yes. "You know he's not mad at us. He just gets mad. Period."

"He took another mental. That's all," Tommy said, leaning over the railing. Mathew came out of his room and hunched himself up beside Martha.

Mathew laughed; it came out nervous and pitched. "I'll see to Martha," he said, reaching over to put his hand on his sister's shoulder.

Martha stood up. "I'm fine. I'm going back to bed now."

Katie stared after them for a full minute as if transfixed on the spot where they had been, then forced herself to reach in her purse for her car keys and leave the house.

Katie turned off Beach Road unto a dirt road and drove for a couple of hours through a thick wooded area before turning back onto the paved highway. So that was his answer to her attempt at discussion. Jeff's message was clear to Katie – *No more talk allowed regarding financial inequalities.* She pushed open the front door and, hearing only the ticking of the grandfather clock in the hall, eased the door shut behind her. She removed her shoes and walked softly down the hall to the den.

In the morning, hearing voices coming from the kitchen, she jerked herself up and straightened her jeans and sweatshirt. Jeff should have been home on a Saturday morning, but she heard only the children talking. She laced up her sneakers, opened the door a few inches and ran quickly toward the hall bathroom. She rubbed her eyes with a dampened washcloth and splashed cold water on her face and neck. Whatever could she say to the kids this time? But, considering the stories they'd been revealing in therapy and their calm the night before, Katie guessed she'd been more alarmed than they.

"Morning," Katie said. Pulling out a chair, she sat down at the kitchen table between Tommy and Martha. "About your father ..." she began but Tommy stopped her.

"We're cool," he said. Head drooping over his bowl, he scooped up the last of his cornflakes and wiped his mouth with a paper napkin. "I'm going to horse around with Matt in the woods for a while."

Martha shifted in her chair in order to face Katie directly. "Everything's okay. Really. No use getting bent out of shape. What you have to do is think about something else right away whenever a bad picture jumps into your head." She tapped her fingers on the table and then retied the bow on her pink flannel nightgown. "Can I make you a piece of toast?" she asked.

"Sure. That would be nice."

Katie watched the girl go to the counter and drop a piece of bread into the toaster and then glance back at her. "You didn't talk to anybody last night, did you?" Martha asked.

"No. I just drove around in the car for quite a while and came home."

"Good." The toast popped up. Martha buttered it, put it on a saucer and brought it to the table. She tugged at her chair to move it closer to Katie. Katie bit into the toast, chewed, and, swallowing hard, forced the doughy half chewed mass down her throat. After another bite, Martha, appearing satisfied, shoved her chair back from the table. "Guess I'll get dressed now."

"Okay, I'm going to make coffee," Katie said. As Martha's slender figure slipped out of the kitchen, Katie remembered Robert McCloskey's unanswered question and wondered – *where do hummingbirds go during a hurricane?*

Katie poured coffee into a mug and drank it slowly, all of it, before getting up and going to the living room.

She ran her hand along the wall across an eight-inch gaping hole and felt its jagged plaster edges under her fingers. This was the same hand that had caressed her so often; the wall's wound almost felt like her wound. She shuddered and feeling disoriented suddenly, backed away from the wall. Stepping between splinters of fractured glass, she yanked all the blinds down to the sills to darken the room. The rest of the day, she stopped herself from looking in there again.

Pacing through the house, imagining knocks at the door, Katie stared out windows. She heated tomato soup for the children's lunch and asked them ordinary questions: Did they want crackers or croutons? Would Martha like to pick out new curtains for her room next week? Was everyone all right? The children eyed her with curiosity as they might have a person babbling in tongues on a street corner. How long could she accommodate herself to the disparate realities of her life, she wondered, before getting stuck in a nowhere place in between?

In the late afternoon, Mathew offered to take his brother and sister out for pizza and a movie. Katie handed over her car keys and some cash, and, as if possessed, asked one more time if everybody was all right. "Of course," Tommy said summoning up what could have been the end of his patience. Not one of them had asked where their father had been all day.

Martha squinted up at Katie. "I, for one, am perfectly fine." She reached for Mathew's hand, then changed her mind, dropped it and ran out the door ahead of her brothers.

As soon as they'd left, Katie realized that without her car she had no means of escape. But by five o'clock, she had decided that Jeff wasn't going to return that evening. Or, forever, maybe? She admitted to causing this tantrum. Jeff must have decided all was well after two and a half weeks of silent compliance since the banister affair.

He would be back eventually; she knew; he wouldn't leave his children in her charge indefinitely. This minute, though, he could be almost anywhere. His company platinum card would transport him to Hong Kong, if that was his pleasure. He'd gone somewhere, at least for the night she felt sure, and that would allow time for her breathing to even out and her arms and shoulders to droop with relief. No longer moving aimlessly, she made herself a cup of tea and started to carry it down the hall toward the den. She could make it through the night, get some sleep and then think what to do next, she decided.

In the next moment, though, the front door latch turned and she ducked quickly into the dining room. She set her cup on the table and huddled against the wall next to the archway in time to watch Jeff's large frame fill the door's entrance.

Never glancing in her direction, he juggled two paper bags in his arms, shut the door with the back of his foot and headed up the stairs. She slipped over to the table and sank into a chair. Her hand went to her chest where she pressed hard and waited.

A few minutes later, she heard him come back down the stairs and walking through the hall. He entered the living room directly across from her and she saw that he wore soiled jeans and an old T-shirt now and carried a shopping bag in each hand. She had a view of him through the dining room archway from her seat at the table, but he gave no indication that he sensed she was there. He stopped in front of the gash and set the bags on the floor, then went to the windows and raised the blinds. Reaching into his bag with a bandaged right hand, he took out a can of white spackling plaster and a spatula knife. Opening the can and shoving the knife into the can, he dug out a glob of white gummy substance and pushed it into the open space. With the gap filled, he scraped the surface again and again with the flat side of the knife. His hands moved almost rhythmically back and forth. Now and then his eyebrows crunched together as he stepped back a foot or two swaying his head side to side to examine his work. Then finally, looking satisfied, almost pleased, Katie thought, appalled, he picked things up, put the empty can and knife back into one of the bags and carted everything down the hall and back upstairs. Evidence gone; subject closed, Katie thought.

Then she heard the shower running. Her hands began to shake, his weird behavior frightening her as much or more than if an intruder had entered their home and wandered about. Like a stuffed animal, Katie sat still in her chair waiting for him to come downstairs again. This time in a fresh shirt and pants, he walked past the dining room to the kitchen. She heard the back door close and the car's engine start up and the car rolling down the driveway. Her body folded into itself, more like a rag doll now. Her head flopped down onto the dining table.

She felt thankful for the sound of the children's voices filling up the silent rooms when they returned from the movie. "We saw *Peter Pan*," Martha said, swinging her head so that her hair flipped to one side, then to the other on her shoulders. This was a new affectation, about a week old. "I loved it. They wanted to go to *True Grit* but I wouldn't."

She had refused; Tommy verified, stood by the ticket window with her hands on her hips and said no.

Good for her, Katie thought, offering them snacks. Martha and Katie had ice cream with cocoa sprinkled on top, Tim opened a bag of Fritos and Mathew poured Cokes.

When the children left to go to their rooms, Katie took a quilt from a linen closet, locked the den door and turned out the lights. Lying on the sofa wide-awake, bedding yanked up to her chin, she waited for the arrival of Sunday morning when she would try to find a way out of this Alice behind the looking glass world in which unbelievably she found herself.

In the morning, she woke to a perfectly quiet house except for a car engine running in the driveway. She ran to the den window, pulled back a drape and watched Jeff and the children backing down the drive in Jeff's black Mercury sedan and turning onto Beach Road.

A while later, drinking coffee she'd just brewed and sitting by a kitchen window with the sun on her back, the events of Friday night – the shuffling noise in the hall, form moving out of the shadows, feet chasing after her, an arm and fist in the air – seemed incongruous. Katie picked up her warm mug with both hands, drank two more cups of coffee and then went outside.

Resurrecting an abandoned lounge chair from under an oily piece of canvas behind the house, she scraped off chunks of paper and dried leaves stuck to its plastic strips and set it up on a patch of brown grass. Fenced in by evergreen bushes and the scraggly pine trees, she stretched out flat and stared up at a blue gray October sky. The chirping of birds in a tree above her were all that broke the quiet. A cool fall breeze swept over her, chilling the bare skin at her throat; she shivered and held her jacket collar tighter at her neck.

She thought about her sister Marijo, tanned and healthy, living in Virginia, happily married with four children now. Katie pictured Sam, Marijo's husband, flipping burgers on an outdoor grill and sipping a cold beer and wondered how Sam would react to Jeff's behavior if he knew. Her brothers, Dennis and Jimmy, also married with kids now. Would they have been disappointed in their perfect little sister for choosing a man like this? Or, would they be only angry and disgusted with Jeff?

Her sister and brothers had never considered divorce, no matter what their marital disagreements. Her older brother John, a monument of strength, ethics and responsibility, now working for NASA in Texas, had been married to Lonny so many years you never said one name without the other. One thing Katie knew for sure: if John suspected for a second that his young sister was in danger, he would come to Rhode Island, pack her belongings and take her far away from here. But how bad was this? Jeff had scared her to death more than once, but he hadn't actually hit her.

Her hand fell to the side of the lounge chair; she picked up a dry blade of grass and stuck it between her teeth. What was the point of crying on shoulders? If she herself didn't understand Jeff's explosions how could she explain them to others? Sharing Jeff's temper rages with her family would give them a lasting impression of him even if he were to get help and change. Is that what she wanted?

Her own fault probably, she admitted now, for marrying a man her family had never laid eyes on. They might have seen what she hadn't. Maxine had believed something about Jeff hadn't wrung true but Katie had blithely brushed off Maxine's concerns. Also her own responsibility, Katie supposed, for not objecting to Jeff's desire to have her all to himself throughout their courtship in California, claiming he didn't want to share their precious little time with her friends or co-workers. Growing up in a large family, no one had ever belonged exclusively to Katie. So when Jeff came along giving her his full attention, keeping everyone at bay, she had to admit to having been seduced by the exclusiveness of their love affair.

She hadn't even objected to their spending nearly all of that first summer in Rhode Island by themselves. The witnesses at their wedding that fall had been strangers coaxed into the parlor by the justice of the peace. Since then, busy with the children, they hadn't nurtured the circle of new friends she'd hoped they would have by now.

Jeff showed no interest in wanting to join her and her *Gazette* co-workers at their local pub and employees at International Computer maintained a safe distance between themselves and their boss and their boss's wife. Jeff, however, seemed in his element at International Computer business receptions and cocktail parties, enjoying his right to place a supportive hand on the shoulder of a subordinate and reveling in their hearty laughter at his jokes. No question, Jeff relished his leadership role and the strict social parameters that accompanied it.

Maxine seemed further away from her than ever on this lonely day. They spoke every few weeks, but Katie hadn't been candid with her friend. God, how Katie wished she could swallow the rock that had lodged in her throat since Friday. She pulled another blade of grass from the ground and bit it in two. A squirrel scuttled through the twigs in front of her, streaked up a tree and perched on a branch. Katie glanced back at the house. Damn, she'd agreed to buy that fortress; she had a right to express her opinion there!

She stood up and, filling her lungs with crisp air, wondered if there was enough oxygen in the universe at the moment to restore her confidence in the future. No question, she was the odd person out in this new family. If she returned to Jeff's bedroom tonight, he would roll over, put his arms around her and tell himself everything is just dandy. How he'd love never having to discuss anything with her ever again.

Chapter Seven

Even more amazing than the early hour was Jeff's cheerful voice at the other end of the phone at 6:30 a.m. on Monday morning. She pictured him in his office, acting like all's well with the world, tilted back in his leather chair, feet crossed and propped up on his desk, a free hand shifting through papers in his lap.

"I came up with an idea on the drive to work," he said. "I think you and I should have an overnight in New York. It would be good for just the two of us to get away from here." He paused. "Are you listening?"

She had lowered herself to a kitchen chair. "This is the first you've spoken to me since Friday. I've been in a terrible state and you want us to have a romantic tryst in New York City? You scared the hell out of me the other night! Am I supposed to forget about that?"

"Don't get hysterical now, Katie. We..."

"No you."

"I realize you're unhappy."

"This isn't about me. I know which of us threw an out of control fit Friday night."

"Come on. Out of control?"

"Was that rational behavior?" *My how pitifully brave I can be on the telephone,* she thought.

"Don't create a drama around this, Katie. We can get Mrs. Lewis to stay overnight with the kids."

"We *have* to talk about your crazy behavior!"

"Got to go now. Meg's motioning to me. Corporate office is on the line. Think about New York, okay?"

If her hand weren't still clutching the receiver, Katie wouldn't believe this call happened. My Lord, Katie thought, realizing that Jeff had already erased the past three days from his mind. If he'd said, "Katie, I don't want to ever act that way again. I'll get help for myself immediately," she might have been a little relieved. But go away with him now?

On the other hand, she certainly wasn't going to risk having a serious talk with him at home. And they couldn't go on living together in silence. And he would act with a cooler head in a public place. No problem with Natalie; she would agree to her taking two days off. *If I were to go it would have to be tonight,* she decided *because I can't sit on this anger for one more day.*

* * * * * * *

Dried leaves crunched under foot as they walked from the airport limo stand on Fifth Avenue to their hotel. The aroma of onions and sausage simmering on a vending cart grill smelled wonderful. Two small children, both girls, in coats and caps skipped alongside a uniformed nanny. Autumn in New York. She and Jeff had planned a trip to New York ever since she'd arrived in Rhode Island. Not under these circumstances, though, Katie recalled with regret.

They crossed 59th Street to the Plaza Hotel and entered the hotel through the grand tearoom with its tall columns, giant potted palms and serving tables loaded with luscious pastries and fresh strawberries and cream. A few minutes later, in their room on the fourth floor, Katie gazed down at the street below where a loving couple boarded one of a line of horse drawn carriages awaiting fresh passengers. She backed away from the window as a waiter in black uniform pushed a linen covered serving table carrying a bottle of cooled champagne and a vase of white roses into the room.

With the champagne popped and the waiter tipped and gone, Jeff lifted the bottle from its silver bucket and filled their glasses.

"To us," he said offering her a glass. "I love you, Katie."

She brought her glass to her lips quickly to hide her discomfort with his efforts to be romantic.

Minutes later, seated at a table in Trader Vic's Polynesian Restaurant on the ground floor, Jeff ordered a bottle of fine Chablis, orange glazed coconut shrimp, wild rice and endive salad for each of them from a waiter in black suit and tie. Jeff was at his best, eyes two glittering stars, mouth curling up suddenly in a smile. His voice rose and fell as he switched from topic to topic: the future home they would one day build together, languages they could learn, countries they would visit.

Katie waited for her first opportunity to bring Jeff back to the point of their getting away together as their waiter returned to pour wine into Jeff's glass. With a flick of his hand, Jeff gave the waiter permission to fill their glasses.

He took a sip while gazing above his glass at Katie. "What's at the top of your wish list?"

"My wish list? For myself you mean?"

"Just for you."

Astonished for a second by the question, she swallowed a sip of wine and answered, "What I've always wanted I suppose. To be happy in my marriage, to publish a periodical, to travel."

He leaned back in his chair looking very much at home. For a moment, she worried he might pull out one of his cigars and light up, but he simply waited for her to continue.

Hurriedly rearranging her thoughts, Katie said, "The publication would have a feminist view. Intelligent but practical," she said and then paused. "I could land on my rear end, of course. Magazines fold every day. I would never be satisfied, though, if I didn't try to do it." To her surprise her own words seemed to be lifting her up in her chair. She reached for her wine glass realizing that her energy had been sapped by too many troublesome matters lately and that she'd gotten way off track.

The waiter placed their salads on the table. "You're right. You have to try," Jeff said. "When we get back, I'll find someone to invest capital in it." He picked up his fork and sampled the salad. "Crisp," he said. "Light olive oil dressing. Taste it."

"Just like that? Now you think you can get capital for me? How?"

"I have some ideas." He pointed to her salad plate. "Eat your salad. Delicate. You'll love it."

"I could start in a modest way. A monthly bulletin at first. Do a mailing." She took three or four bites of salad. "I could write the first issue blindfolded. I've been planning it so long." Her spirits now soaring with possibilities, she smiled. "I can do this – I mean I can if you get help to curtail your anger because I can't think coherently while I'm waiting for you to explode again." She waited a second or two, then added, "You must be under a great deal of pressure, Jeff. We should find out why."

He smiled at her. "I'll do it if you think that it will help you to relax."

"Jeff, it's for your own good. And for your kids too."

"Sure, I'll do it."

"You will?"

"Yes."

"For certain, Jeff?"

"Yes."

"Do you want me to try to find a good therapist for you?"

"No. I'll do it myself."

Jeff reached for a piece of French bread from a bowl, spread butter on it and grinned back at her. "I'm thinking we can fix up one of our unused bedrooms. Then your hours can be flexible while you're working. That way the kids will be supervised and safe and we'll both have piece of mind."

"But Mrs. Lewis is already there after school for the kids."

"In which case, we would only need her one day a week to do some cleaning."

"No," Katie said, having learned that it was important to try to stay ahead of Jeff. He didn't understand how absorbed she'd have to be in this project. "Absolutely, I would need an office away from the house. A small one to start with. I would have to do this in a serious way. You know how much I've always wanted this. I've talked about it since we first met."

He searched her face, looking for the weak link in her chain of reasoning, she guessed. The waiter took away their salad dishes and returned with the shrimp entree and rice. Katie ate with a good appetite for the first time in four days.

Jeff appeared subdued for a few minutes, but the dinner revived him and before long he was conversing full speed again. "Next summer, we should take a trip to Spain and to France the following year," he said.

Pouring cream over his plump strawberries, he leaned back in his chair for a moment as if studying her. "You're sparkling. I want you to succeed. I hope you know that."

"Way deep down, I think you do." She reached across the table and let him grasp her hand and then smiled at him.

Back in their room Katie wandered over to the windows and glanced down at Fifth Avenue this time. Jeff followed her, reached both arms around her waist from behind and set his cheek softly against hers. To her surprise, some of the old warm feelings swept over her. *This is how I'd hoped our marriage would be,* she remembered, *the two of us slipping off somewhere to revitalize ourselves every so often.* She was glad she hadn't burdened anyone with her troubles. *When he gets real help for his temper we can try to solve our own problems.*

She turned around and he brushed the hair back from her forehead. "I'm so glad you came to New York with me. I've felt miserable the past few days," he said.

"That makes two of us."

Placing his hands at her waist, he brought her closer to him and kissed her gently on her lips. Then he ran his hand down the zipper at her back and she let her dress slip down over her hips and legs to the floor. She shivered for an instant, and then assured herself: *He's going to get better. I'm going to believe in him again.*

They sank onto the bed and came together, lips brushing over eyelids and ears. Warm skin touching warm skin, hands massaging, holding, caressing, they clung to one another. Her body turned to melting liquid at its center as he lifted her up to his kisses – fluid washing away stress, undoing fear. They came together releasing tension, for Katie, more an act of hope and promise than rapture. Jeff rolled over carrying her with him, arms still around her holding her in his grasp. Before falling asleep, he whispered, "No matter what, never doubt how much I love you, Katie."

She nestled into the curve of his chest, a voice inside her crying softly: *I could still love him if only...if only...*

Chapter Eight

Jeff had maintained his cheerful mood all week since their trip to New York and Katie had begun to research the first steps needed to start a new publication. And that evening at the table after dinner with the kids already in their rooms, Katie decided to pick up on their conversation where they had left off in New York.

"Have you tried to find a good therapist yet?" she asked Jeff.

He smiled at her before answering. "Not yet. But aren't we doing just fine now? Why not leave well enough alone, Katie?"

Alarmed, she said, "But how long will this last? I'm feeling better because of your promise to get help. In the past I've thought things had improved only to have your mood change. And now I'm afraid you'll blow up again."

"Okay. I'll do it. I'll do it. But don't bug me about it, please."

"All right. I'll change the subject. Have you thought any more about financial backing for my periodical? I'm so anxious to get started on it."

"Damn, Katie, stop nagging. Settle back for a while. Relax, will you? Try to be happy now that we're fine."

She questioned her own memory for a second, wondering whether she had made it all up, New York, their conversation, their agreements. After a long pause, she said, "Jeff, I can't wait forever for you to keep promises you make to me,"

"I didn't say forever." He jerked himself up from his chair, knocking over his glass; water splashed across the kitchen table. He stomped out of the room toward the den where he flipped on the television.

Speechless, Katie stayed seated and gazed dumbly after him.

After that night, Jeff's rages started to occur on a regular basis without warning. He threw whatever was close enough to grab – dishes, potted plants, lamps. Though he hadn't attacked her personally, Katie ran from the house often, drove south on Beach Road, and pulled into a parking lot facing the water. At odd hours, hers was the only car there. Resting her head on the seatback, she watched folds of white foam roll up over the sand and slip back into the ocean.

How many ways had she phrased her polite inquiries: "I found out the name of someone good, Jeff." "Did you call the Therapist's Network?" "Can I call them for you?" As far as Katie was concerned, his sudden flare-ups could have been incited by a full moon, the ebb and flow of the earth's tides, pins in a voodoo doll...

Then one day she realized that he had begun to introduce her to people in a new way that chilled her from the inside out: "I'd like you to meet my lovely wife who 'used to live in San Francisco' or 'used to work at *New Times* magazine'; or 'used to... well, just about anything'," he would say as though she'd ceased to be of interest in her present form. He never said, "This is my wife who is a feature writer at the *Gazette*." At other times he said, "This isn't like you," when she'd done something that was exactly like her. She felt he was denying whole parts of her, trying to mould her into someone she wasn't. Sometimes, though, she had trouble recognizing herself. She'd begun to couch her sentences in precautionary language that midstream seemed to sprout little angel wings that lifted her words up at the finish transforming what had started out as a statement into a timid question.

Her job and the children seemed the only things fastening her to the earth's surface. Breezing into the newsroom, Katie filled her coffee mug and started in on her latest assignment each morning. One afternoon a week, she picked up the kids and drove them to another of their clandestine sessions with Dr. Henry. Their therapist disapproved vigorously of her continuing to live with Jeff, warning her constantly that she was in personal danger. And yet, she didn't leave. She worried what would happen to the kids. She knew her marriage was going up in smoke, or more accurately, turning into a four alarm fire. Still she didn't leave. She had quit having pipedreams in which Charlene regains custody of the kids or Jeff is cured. Katie felt trapped by a fear of taking action that having set in gradually like the drip drip of a leaky faucet could soon fill a bathtub.

Suddenly Jeff started to moan about the possibility that one day he would lose his children. "Robert will graduate soon from Boston University and take off for a job in New York or elsewhere," he would say. "And, in another year, Mathew will enroll at the University of Rhode Island. Who knows what the hell Tommy will do – sail off to Tahiti maybe," he ranted. "And Martha, she's already asking to do high school at a prep boarding school. Why can't they stay here and go to a college nearby?"

Katie's honest answer to that question would have sent him into a tailspin. In her opinion, Jeff would have locked all of them up in his palace forever and thrown away the key if he could have arranged it. In a frantic effort to hang on to his kids, he started to take them with him on business trips whenever possible, staying at the Plaza in New York, Four Seasons in Toronto, the Ambassador in Los Angeles. The kids didn't say how they felt about the constant traveling and spending hours in hotel rooms, but, as usual, they complied with their dad's wishes.

Katie liked not having to predict Jeff's erratic moods for a couple of days at a time. Except that an ominous calm seemed to settle over the old mansion when everyone was away. Shadows reached out from the corners of rooms; the spindly pine trees out back scraped wilder on the panes, making her slap at them through the window. One evening, her anxiety got the best of her and she called Natalie asking her if she'd like to meet somewhere for dinner.

"Sure, and I'll call Steve to join us," she said. "How about the Catch of the Day Pub?"

"Good, I think I know where it is," Katie said.

Katie looked forward to talking with Steve and Natalie outside the office. From her first day at the *Gazette* she'd been comfortable with both of them. Natalie's sense of humor and Steve's unassuming manner gave Katie a connection to the sort of people and a world she'd left behind in San Francisco.

Katie spotted Steve waving to her from a window booth at the far end of the open beamed pub. A mile outside of Barrington Village, the Catch of the Day was well hidden from the highway by a forest of evergreen trees and, having escaped the attention of tourists, had remained a cherished local meeting place. Katie dashed across the wide plank floor and slipped into a wooden booth across from Steve and alongside Natalie.

"We ordered fish and chips and a side of coleslaw for all of us," Natalie said.

"Let's have a beer first," Steve suggested.

"Good idea," Katie agreed. "Nice to relax for an evening with Jeff and the kids away. Otherwise I rush home, check who needs what, eat a quick supper with Jeff and help the kids with homework."

"Join us more often," Natalie said.

Steve waved to a friend at the bar and held up three fingers to a woman in jeans and T-shirt. "An exclusive club, Katie," he said. "Behave, and we might sponsor you for permanent membership."

The waitress set three beer bottles on the table. "How's everybody tonight?"

"Gracie, this is Katie," Natalie said.

"Hey, nice to meet you." Gracie smiled and shoved a pencil behind her ear. "Give a holler when you want your food."

Katie picked up her icy cold beer and took a long drink. "So I've gathered both of you are happy living here in idyllic Barrington Village?"

"Not a bad life for the boonies. Hiking in the woods. Gazing at the ocean. Discussing the state of the world in our favorite hangout. What's not to like?"

"And the *Gazette* is a good place to work," Katie said.

"True, but the *Gazette* is only my day job." Steve took another drink and set down his bottle. "I'm writing a novel in my spare time." He smiled. "Well, at least that's my excuse for living in la-la land. To maintain credibility, I peck at the manuscript now and then."

"I guess you can live anywhere you choose to, Steve?" Katie asked. She hoped he wouldn't think she was getting too personal, but she was curious.

Steve pushed a clump of his thick dark hair back from his forehead. "Well, I almost ended up in New York when I finished college. But I changed my mind."

Natalie dug a cigarette out of her purse, lit it and then peered over the lit cigarette at Steve. "And then he backed out of a marriage proposal and came here instead." She took a long drag and blew the smoke away from the table.

"Don't listen to her. That's not how it was." Steve held his bottle in front of his face as if seriously examining its label. "Ginny and I realized we wanted different things from life. That's all. Sweet kid. I still think of her as a kid, but she's nearly thirty-five now. Works at an ad agency in New York."

Katie ran two fingers down the side of her frosty bottle. "Good thing you discovered that beforehand. It's difficult to learn things about a person after you're married." Steve sat up straighter, the way he often did when working on a story that had moved him. His best work portrayed the lives of the invisible people who cleaned the oceanfront summer homes and manicured the miles of grass carpet that surrounded them. "A general observation," Katie added quickly.

Steve set his beer on the table. "Glad to hear that. A good journalist is always observant."

"Thank you."

"Say, I've been meaning to ask if you'd like to work on a series with me," he said.

"What's the series?" Katie asked, as if she wouldn't be thrilled to work with Steve on anything.

"Single mothers coming here to live more cheaply than in the city, then finding themselves the member of a captive work force at the bottom of the wage scale."

"I'll do it." She answered too eagerly but what of it, her fingernails were tingling at the prospect. "I'd like to sink my teeth into something purposeful." Now her stomach was doing flip-flops the way it used to at *New Times* when she'd been handed a good assignment.

"I'm glad you two have taken the burden off the editor-in-chief to make a decision here," Natalie said. "I'm in favor, but who asked?"

Steve grinned at Natalie. "Come on. I knew you'd agree."

Natalie raised an eyebrow. "Oh, really?"

Katie viewed their little dance with interest. "Can you two read each other's minds?"

"Two old war buddies," Steve commented.

"No more shoptalk." Natalie rolled her eyes. "I want you to know I had a cool weekend away from this Garden of Eden."

Steve glanced over at her. "Seems you're spending a lot of time in the Big Apple lately."

"Saw *Man from La Mancha*, heard some fine R&B and had a nice visit with my family."

Steve tipped his bottle, pointing the nozzle straight at Natalie. "Come on, Nat. You're holding back."

"I suppose you tell me everything about your private life?"

"Not much to tell at the moment." He took another drink. "Other than how I'm enjoying myself."

"Well, that's all anybody is getting from me," Natalie announced. "With my blood sugar down, I might reveal more than I want to. Let's have another beer and ask for our food."

Katie wanted to know a lot more about her colleagues, but decided not to probe too much on their first night out together.

Other than time spent with her friends Steve and Natalie when Jeff was away, all that winter Katie daydreamed about leaving her belongings behind in Barrington, driving off somewhere, anywhere, destination unknown, in her car. She used to think people were spineless for tossing away marriages like empty milk cartons, but ending a marriage now seemed to take more courage than staying. She believed she might still love Jeff, but an angry lead weight in the pit of her stomach said she hated him too. The last thing he cared about when he blew up was whether she was doubled over in terror. No question, his fury was directed at her. She was more occupied with her job than with him, causing her to fuck up constantly at home, he said. She had stopped reminding him of all *he* wasn't doing to help at home. Why induce another rampage? The thought never entered her mind anymore.

The ground under her feet seemed to have lost its consistency, forcing her to take smaller and smaller steps to keep from slipping backward. And looking too far ahead on the path appeared downright foolhardy. She felt incapacitated by her new found timidity, her loyalty to the kids and by her remaining, but barely flickering, embers of affection for Jeff. And she'd become less and less comfortable sleeping with him curled up to her body. Making love with him left her feeling hollow and more dishonest with each passing week.

One morning out of sheer desperation, Katie decided to place another call to Charlene even though Jeff's ex-wife had never returned her calls in the past. "Steve, tell Natalie when she gets off the phone that I'll be right back," Katie said before heading out the door and walking down the street toward the nearest outside payphone.

"This is Katie," she stammered when, for the first time, a woman actually answered Charlene's phone.

"I hope for your sake Jeff doesn't know you're calling me," Charlene said immediately.

"Of course not," Katie answered while resting her shoulder against the phone booth window. "Thanks for picking up."

"Are the children okay?" Charlene asked in a trembling voice.

Katie tried to choose her words carefully. "Yes. For the moment, at least. But now that you and I are finally talking I'm not sure what to say. The problem is Jeff's temper and other things too. I don't know how much longer I can..."

"Why is he still angry?" Charlene broke in. "He wore me down until he got the children. What else could he want?"

With her forehead now pressed hard to the phone booth glass, Katie asked, "Are you afraid of him?" She bit her lip waiting for Charlene's response, although, with Jeff's present actions and the children's accounts in therapy, she already guessed what Charlene's answer would be.

"I was," Charlene whispered into the phone. "But I'm no threat to him now."

"What would happen if I left him? I mean to the children? I've been almost totally responsible for them," Katie said, her own voice quivering now. "He's so volatile. Nothing helps; he's never satisfied." She felt ready to dissolve into a teary mess during her first ever conversation with Charlene, but she continued anyway. "I try to please him," Katie said. Suddenly her own comment pulled up an instant flashback to her old Berkeley women's group and their theories about *those women* who tried too hard to please husbands while losing themselves in the process. She saw the arrogance of those views now and felt ashamed that they had felt themselves immune to falling into such a trap.

"I can't get the children back from Jeff," Charlene said. "He'd buy himself an expensive lawyer. And if the courts did give me custody again, Jeff would be enraged. I don't know what he might do." Charlene was the one crying now. "He assured me again and again that he'd gotten his anger under control before marrying you. I tortured myself asking why he had done this for you when I could never persuade him to get help. He told me again and again that you were anxious to have the children with you and him, and finally I buckled. I was terrified all the time back then. He ordered me to screen your calls and not to answer the messages you left. By the time I felt safe, you had stopped calling me."

"I didn't ask your children to live with us. I didn't even know they were coming until they were here. Please don't think I would have done that."

Feeling exhausted and suddenly more hopeless than ever, Katie wanted only to get off the phone. "I'll keep you posted but I have to do something soon. I wanted you to know that. I'll call you about the kids soon of course," she said.

Holding onto the phone booth door handle for support, Katie hung up and gazed numbly out the window. Charlene had just dissipated Katie's best hope for a way out that wouldn't jeopardize the children.

Then she gasped: *Oh, my God, Charlene believed I had wanted to steal her children.* Yes, she admitted now, *so many coincidences – her own move to Rhode Island, buying the home with multiple bedrooms, Charlene's exodus, would have had to occur for all of these kids to end up under my roof.*

She wiped the tears from her cheeks with the sleeve of her jacket. And yet, accepting such gross duplicity on Jeff's part was excruciating for her, even now. To do so would mean questioning every conversation she and Jeff had had before their wedding and since then. Surely their whirlwind, romantic courtship had been genuine. Why choose her in particular if all he wanted was a woman to keep the home fires burning for him and his kids?

In California, Jeff had teased her about her independent spirit and praised her ambition. He knew what he was getting, didn't he? She pushed herself away from the window glass and lowered herself to the corner seat in the phone booth. A dreadful understanding was unfolding in her mind: *What Jeff had wanted from the start was everything: an earth mother, a devoted wife, an interesting, intelligent woman – the last expectation coming with a qualifier: as long as his wife's goals didn't interfere with his own.* Katie swallowed hard. Jeff had been giving her serious side glances lately as if asking himself: "Is she measuring up?" "Filling all these pairs of shoes without losing any of her original luster?" Above all, not "letting herself go?"

Katie dropped her head to her chest. *I can't be all these women,* she whispered into her hands. *I don't want to be spread that thin. I would have told you so, Jeff. If you'd only been honest with me. Stop the music now. Stop it! I'm already dancing as fast as I can.*

* * * * * * *

On her way to work the next day Katie glanced out her car window at the ocean and heaved a generous sigh. Dew off the water seeped through the small opening in her driver's side window. The snow was gone except for small patches clinging to brown grass alongside the road. Yes, summer was returning, but the thought of squeezing another somewhat tranquil three months of sailing out of Jeff seemed improbable.

Minutes later, when she entered the newsroom, Steve greeted her with a multicolored bouquet of spring flowers. "Thank you," she stammered, dropping her bag on her desk to accept them. "What? Why?"

"To see you smile."

Natalie interrupted from her office across the walkway. "Hey, Steve," she announced, "I'll laugh my head off if you give me a dozen roses."

"Okay, I promise," Steve answered.

"I'm stunned," Katie said. She sat down to admire her gift and to appreciate her friend Steve who was pulling up a chair next to her desk. She brought the flowers closer to inhale their delicate sweetness. She had often wondered how she might feel about Steve if she weren't married to Jeff. But this morning the question seemed unnecessary. She would have been taken with Steve under any circumstances. She swiveled around in her chair to face him.

"Do you know you've been at the *Gazette* a year and a half today?" he said.

"Honest? But why would you remember a thing like that?"

"I don't know, except that on my way to work this morning I was thinking about you and how you've covered stories from the governor's press conferences to cornering ice cream vendors holding fake licenses at the beach and everything in between since you've been here. And then I realized I haven't heard you mention your dream of publishing your own periodical lately." He took a sip from his coffee mug. "Those kids are a little older now and should be getting more responsible. Might be easier to start the magazine than it seemed earlier."

"Honestly, Steve, I used to believe my life was charmed. Thought I could do anything I wanted to. Maybe my magic has lost its power."

"You have to recharge magic every so often. Don't you know that?" He rested back in his chair, obviously in one of his thoughtful moods. "You'd do a terrific job with a magazine."

She frowned. "I don't have the capital I'd need. A little savings is all I've got. And Jeff has so many other obligations." She added this quickly, sure that would be Steve's next question.

"I'll bet together, you and I could come up with some backing." He leaned slightly forward. "Want a silent partner?"

She broke into a broad smile. "What? You would do that?"

"Love to," he said. He stood up. "Let's talk about it later."

On a day that had started out unbelievably dreary, Steve had managed to lift her spirits. How she'd like to be truthful with him and Natalie about her personal life, but then, what was the truth? That Jeff had fits, but never mind, perhaps they were the result of bad childhood experiences? Or, maybe they were caused by some untreated mental illness? What did she herself believe? And how could she explain Jeff's ability to control himself in public but not with her? Most likely these new friends of hers would think her a fool for claiming to still love him at all. And worst of all, they would think less of her personally, she was sure, for staying with him. Either of these outcomes seemed intolerable at the moment. Her colleague-friends' respect was what got her out of bed every morning.

She clicked on her keyboard to finish a story she'd been working on the night before and then smiled. *Imagine Steve bringing those lovely flowers?*

A while later, Steve sauntered back to her desk. "How would you like to co-author another series with me?" he asked. "On domestic violence, legal matters, profile of abusers, safe houses. What the community is doing for the victims."

Stalling for time, Katie opened a drawer and took out a memo pad, then ran her fingers through her hair and took in a large breath. Disgusted with her own hesitation, she summoned up her most forceful voice. "Sure. This story is overdue."

* * * * * * *

Steve parked near a small frame house nestled in a wooded area several miles from Barrington Village. Jean Warren, a tall wiry middle-aged woman, met them at the front door and introduced herself as director of the shelter. She ushered them into a parlor off a narrow hall. "Two women have agreed to talk with you. You can't use names of course," she reminded them before leaving the room.

Katie lowered herself onto a well-worn sofa, then took a Kleenex from her purse and wiped her damp palms. For heaven's sake, she hadn't felt this nervous before an interview since her first days out of journalism school.

Jean came back with a girl in sweatshirt and jeans, hair combed back from her forehead forming a ponytail in back. A baby, about a year old, rested on her hip, two chubby legs wrapped around his mother's waist. She took a seat in a rocker while Steve introduced himself and Katie to her.

Flipping open a notebook, Steve said, "We'll try to make this as easy as possible."

The baby made a humming noise and his mother took a pacifier from her jeans pocket and placed it in his mouth. "I'm not sure what you want to know."

"Whatever comes to mind," Steve answered. "How old you are. How long you've been married."

"My husband is twenty, I'm nineteen. We were married two years in August." She smoothed the baby's fine blond hair. "He's a fisherman. Gone at dawn every day, in every kind of weather. I never know what time he'll get back."

Katie thought how such an undependable schedule would have given Jeff an anxiety attack. "Must be difficult to plan things," Katie said.

"Oh, yes," the girl answered. "But still he wants his meal on the table the minute he walks in the door." She strummed her fingers on the arm of the rocker. "I have to heat it up, but sometimes I have to stop to do something for the baby."

"And this makes him angry?" Katie said. She undid the top button of her shirt where she felt herself getting warm.

"Yes. That's what gets him started. That's usually when he smacks me."

Steve moved forward in his chair. Katie expected him to leap to his feet and throw his arms around the girl's shoulders. But instead, he asked her, "How often does this happen?"

"At least twice a week, maybe more," she answered. "I was holding Bobby the other night when my husband slapped me so hard I dropped the baby. I was scared out of my wits he might be hurt. After eating, my husband fell asleep on the couch and I grabbed Bobby and his diaper bag and ran over to my neighbor's home next door. I wasn't thinking. I just went. My neighbor called her Baptist Church. A woman from the church brought us here." The girl tightened her arms around her baby.

"What would you like to do now?" Katie asked, then seeing the girl's puzzled expression, realized how naïve her question must have sounded – as if this young woman had unending options.

"Go to where he won't follow us. Get a job. I used to be a supermarket checkout girl. But, someone will have to watch Bobby for me. I think about this stuff all night while other people are sleeping." She leveled her eyes at Katie. "I don't expect you to do anything special to help me. But do you have any suggestions about what *I* can do?" She jiggled the baby on her lap.

"Our series in the paper will make people more aware of what you're facing," Katie said. Seeing the girl's doubtful look again, she added hurriedly, "I know you need practical help right away. We'll publish a phone number for people to offer assistance." Katie turned hopefully to Steve. Their previous solutions didn't seem as brilliant here as they had back in the newsroom.

"We'll do what we can," he said. "There may be private organizations that can offer help."

"All I need is daycare and a little place to live. I would move anywhere. Maybe back to New Bedford, Massachusetts where I grew up." The baby fidgeted in her lap and whined through his pacifier. "It's time for him to eat. In a minute he'll be howling." She stood up shifting him back to her hip. "I'm supposed to leave here by next week. I'm Kelly. I guess Mrs. Warren will know where I am."

"Good," Katie said, while feeling she'd been absolutely useless to the girl. "We'll be in touch. Thanks for talking with us."

Minutes later, Jean appeared with the other woman, perhaps in her fifties, short dark hair, wearing a stylish pantsuit, a scarf at her neck. Shades of blue and purple circled one of her eyes; the eyelid was maroon where stitches had apparently been taken. She sat down next to Katie on the sofa. "I never talk about this," she said, "but there's no reason not to now. I'm leaving my husband of twenty-five years." She gazed down at the floor. "He's a cardiologist at Providence Hospital," she whispered, as though letting go of a long kept secret. "Everyone thought he was a fine family man. My daughter and I knew differently."

"How long has the abuse been going on?" Katie asked, wishing she could get up and open a window to let in some fresh air.

"At first he yelled and threw tantrums. One day, he clamped his hand to the back of my neck and made me read aloud from a list of instructions he'd written for me." She raised her hands and covered her face. "This is difficult." She cleared her throat. "The pushing and shoving started after that. Then worse."

Steve, visibly shaken now, offered to get the woman some water. She said no thank you and Katie waited for him to ask what she sensed would be his next question.

"Why do you think you stayed with him?"

"We've had beautiful times together. I had loved him for so long I never even questioned if the love was still there.

'Never again', he always said. I started to believe *I* was the problem. When someone tells you that often enough, it starts to take shape in your head." Seeming baffled, she went silent for a moment and then shook her head. "Strange, because I'm strong-willed everywhere else."

"What will you do now?" Steve asked her.

"Stay with my daughter in Chicago temporarily." She stood up and straightened her jacket. "I'll shed my tears after the plane has left the runway. A lot of them."

Steve leaped to his feet. "Best to you. Thank you for talking with us." He reached for her hand. "At this difficult time."

Steve plopped his notebook on a counter in a nearby diner. "We'll do a good job on this, Katie. Tomorrow, you can find out how many shelters there are in the state. Jean Warren says there's a waiting list to get in." He took a bite of his sandwich, giving Katie a closer look. "You're being quiet." He picked up his iced tea. "This was disturbing for me, too."

"I'm all right." Katie shoved her plate aside and took a long swallow of ice water. "I'm not hungry. I'll take the sandwich with me." She felt ridiculously on the verge of tears. She'd conducted many interviews as disheartening as this one and kept her objective distance. Sure, Jeff had his explosions, but he hadn't laid a hand on her she reminded herself, but then at once she recalled Dr. Henry's dire warnings. The inside of her mouth suddenly felt like sandpaper. She picked up her glass, drank the rest of her water and glanced back at Steve. "Don't worry, I'll be professional." She straightened herself up on the stool and pulled back her shoulders. "We got two good interviews. Three, counting Jean Warren's. And we can use every word of them."

Steve stuck his notebook into his suit coat pocket. "We can start the phone calls right away."

"I have an appointment with Judge Andrews at Family Court tomorrow. That should be enlightening," Katie said, making a stab at sounding more businesslike than she was feeling.

"Let's find out if they track these restraining orders in any useful way," Steve said.

She wrapped a napkin around her sandwich and stuck it in her purse. "We'll do a good job on this series, Steve."

"How did the interview go?" Natalie called out from her office when they returned, then came out to Katie's desk.

"Fine, I believe." Katie's eyes followed Steve back to his desk where he had already reached for his phone. "People open up to him, don't they? They sense how much he cares."

Natalie smiled. "You say that as though caring were something remarkable."

"I'm not that cynical, but I think people back off when they feel powerless to change things. Not Steve, he keeps on battling his windmills. Hardly ever gets discouraged." She dropped her notes and purse onto her desk. "I used to be like that. Super idealistic."

"You still are. That's why you two are such a good team."

Katie smiled. "Really?"

Chapter Nine

Katie kicked off her shoes and stretched out on the bed. A little rest is all she needed before leaving for her Media Women's meeting that evening. She was feeling good about the response she and Steve had received to their domestic violence series. They'd had a tentative promise of greater financial commitment from state government and offers of help from a respected charitable organization and a few Rhode Island corporations. She'd even been able to get a department store sales job for Kelly and find her a studio apartment and a babysitter in New Bedford, Massachusetts. One case out of so many, but helping Kelly had given Katie some personal gratification.

After a short nap, she got up from the bed, shed her work clothes and changed into a black silk blouse and a white wool suit. Smoothing the pantyhose on her legs, she slipped on a pair of sling back patent leather pumps, brushed her long hair and ran a pink lipstick over her lips.

Downstairs she pinned a note – "Gone to Press and Media Women's Association meeting at the Ship's Tavern Restaurant" – to the refrigerator. She took in a breath of crisp night air before getting into her car and suddenly realized how much she was looking forward to the evening. If her sources were correct, the members were going to ask her to serve as next year's chairwoman for their Barrington chapter.

* * * * * * *

"Hey, I have some big news!" Katie announced breathlessly two hours later when she burst into the kitchen where Jeff stood by the counter pouring himself a glass of orange juice.

"So you were out at the Ship's Tavern with your girl friends while I was cooling my heels at the airport?" he said.

"Wasn't your car at the airport? You couldn't get a cab?"

"I got a cab after waiting twenty minutes."

"Well, you're safe and sound now. I told you about my Women's Media Association meeting before you left for New York on Wednesday. The meeting was terrific, by the way. They appointed me chairwoman of our chapter..."

"Shove your meeting," he growled before ripping his arm back and letting go of his glass. A second later, the glass slammed into the refrigerator door spurting frothy liquid and tiny glass fragments across the room.

"Damn," she screamed. "Stop throwing things. Stop threatening me! I'm sick of it."

"You are?" He snapped his arm back again bending his elbow and pulling his fist to the side.

Get away from him, back up a voice screamed in her head as she staggered to the side to dodge him. She dashed toward the back door but his leg rose up and his shoe caught her ankle. She tripped and fell to the floor but dragged herself up and regaining her balance, sprang forward toward the door again. He grabbed her with one hand on her shoulder this time and, pulled back his other hand to strike her. She jumped aside but not in time to avoid his hand hitting her cheek. Yanking up her briefcase from the counter she slapped it across his face. Then she whipped around and ran out the door. She stumbled on the back steps and jettisoned forward onto the rough stone surface of the path face first scraping her cheek and hands and knees.

Hearing the back door open behind her, she forced herself to get up again and ran to her car. Leaping into the driver's seat, she pulled the door shut and smacked down the lock button. Grasping at the keys in her purse now dangling by a shoulder strap from her neck, she turned the ignition, raced down the driveway and made a fast right turn onto the highway.

But, my God, where could she go? Her first thought was to drive to Natalie's but it was too late to wake her. Maybe there was a safe place to park at the beach and sleep in her car, she thought. But she kept heading south, almost unaware of where she was going until she turned onto the dirt road that led to the women's shelter.

Jean Warren answered her knock at the door at once. "Mrs. O'Connell!" she said. "Whatever? Come in."

Katie smacked her hand to her mouth. "Quick. I'm going to vomit," she warned Jean.

Jean rushed ahead of her. "Follow me. The bathroom is down the hall."

Katie gagged into the toilet until there was nothing left inside her and then wiped the blood from her face with a washcloth that Jean handed to her. "I'm so sorry," she said. "I didn't know where else to go. I feel like such a fool."

"Don't be embarrassed, Mrs. O'Connell. I promise you're not the first professional woman or wife of a prominent man to come here. Let's go upstairs."

"I'm not a hypocrite, Jean. I *didn't* believe he would ever do this." *But what, then, have I been afraid of, time after time,* she asked herself. *Why was I so often barely able to swallow or breathe right with my stomach in knots?*

"Just sit there." Jean pointed to a foldout cot in a small upstairs bedroom. "He's been violent before this, hasn't he? They always have."

"Yes, but not...oh, never mind. I'm so sorry." Katie sat on the cot clutching her purse in one hand and told Jean what she could remember about what had happened.

"Wait here. I'm going to get you a glass of water," Jean told her.

"Does somebody guard this place?" Katie asked when Jean returned.

"We can't afford twenty-four-hour security, but a Barrington patrol car drives by off and on during the night. I can call them directly any time, of course." She put her hand on Katie's shoulder. "You're safe here. You're lucky you got away. You'll be hurting and stressed out for a time, but please don't see your husband under any circumstances and do not let him know where you are. Please, don't go back to him if he apologizes on bended knee. I'll be back in a minute with a nightshirt."

Katie couldn't imagine Jeff saying he was sorry outright like that. The matter of guilt had always hung there waiting to be claimed after one of his explosions. Without an apology from him, Katie had been left to mull over how much of his latest temper fit she had caused. Promises he made after a rampage always left her feeling that he was the one doing the forgiving.

She glanced around the tiny room. Another cot was made up across from hers and there were clothes hanging in a portable closet. "Everyone here is sworn to confidentiality, right?" she asked when Jean came back to the room. She sounded like Martha and she knew it, only she wasn't sure whom she was trying to protect: the children? Jeff? Herself?

"Don't worry, this is a secret society. We respect everyone's privacy." Jean glanced at the other cot. "I'll see that your roommate doubles up down the hall tonight. She'll move back in here sometime tomorrow. You'll hear children in the morning, too. There are four kids with us at the moment."

Katie reached for the nightshirt Jean had set on her cot and started to unbutton her white wool jacket. "Shit," she said, touching the streaks of dirt mixed with blood on the front of it. "I bought this suit. He didn't." She yanked off the jacket and threw it on the floor.

"A ruined suit isn't your biggest problem right now though, is it?" Jean said.

"No, but it's one I can understand. Can I ask you a favor, Jean?" She dug into her purse and pulled out Dr. Henry's card. "Will you call this Dr. Henry for me? Tell him why I'm here, please." She kicked off her sling back pumps.

"Sure. Get undressed and lie down now." Jean patted Katie's hand. "Try to sleep."

In the dark, Katie gazed out a tiny window at a black starless night and whispered into her pillow, "Maxine, old friend, it looks as if I *really* forgot to cover my ass this time as you had insisted I do. She rolled over on the lumpy foldout cot mattress, turning her body to protect the side hurting the most. *Where will I go when I leave here? God, what have I done? I should have known this would finally happen. How stupid I've been. How stupid!*

The early sunlight through the tiny window woke her, but she had only slept fitfully anyway. *I have never felt this alone; I need help and I need a friend,* she had admitted to herself at about 4:00 a.m. Even if she choked on her embarrassment, she decided to call Natalie in the morning and tell her the truth.

At 9:00 a.m. she pulled on a sweatshirt and a pair of jeans that Jean had brought her and asked if she could use the office phone.

Natalie, already at the *Gazette*, thank God, answered her own phone. Katie hoped she could describe the circumstances to Natalie in some sort of rational manner without breaking down completely.

"Katie, where are you?" Natalie asked her. "You're never late for work."

"I'm in so much trouble. I don't know where to start. Please believe me when I tell you I'm sorry to involve you. But I don't know where else to turn."

"What the hell happened?"

"Let me tell you where I am. I'm at the women's shelter. I had to come here last night. It was Jeff, he... Could you come to see me at lunchtime, please? I'll tell you anything you want to know then."

"I'm in shock, Katie. Yes, I'll be there, of course. Try to hold yourself together till then."

Natalie arrived with her own attorney, Fran Marconi, a petite woman, dark hair parted down the middle and hanging straight the way Maxine used to wear hers. The attorney had on a gray skirt and jacket and Katie wondered if her old pal Maxine was also wearing suits in San Francisco these days.

"Tell us what you can," Natalie said, interrupting Katie's meandering thoughts.

Katie swallowed hard and began. "He's displayed a bad temper for a long time, but last night he really tried to hurt me." They listened to the rest of Katie's story with stunned expressions, uttering empathetic sounds every now and then. Fran took notes throughout while Natalie held onto Katie's hand.

At the end, Natalie said, "I can hardly speak. I can't believe Jeff... he seemed such a gentleman."

"All right," Fran said. "Here's what we have to do. We'll get a restraining order against your husband. I can get you a temporary one delivered tomorrow. We'll go to court later for a permanent one."

Katie tried to pay attention, but Fran's voice kept fading in and out. "Hand me that glass of water, Natalie, please," Katie said. She wished she could flip a switch and make the room go dark again. Her chest throbbed as she reached for her purse on the nightstand. She set the purse on her stomach and felt around inside until she found her little good luck elephant. Running her hand over the smooth back, her fingers moved tentatively to its broken foot and rested there.

Fran, sitting at the end of the cot, shifted through papers on her lap, and, flattening two sheets on her briefcase, handed a pen to Katie. "Sign each of these at the bottom."

"What does this do?"

"It tells Jeff not to come near you when you leave here."

"I don't know how he'll react. His reputation will suffer from this. Damn, why did he have to turn into a crazy person? We could have been happy." Katie's voice trailed off and she started to cry and then began to sob with her whole body. Fran dropped her briefcase on the floor and reached her arms around Katie.

"Do you have a valium?" Natalie asked Fran.

"Yes, in my briefcase," Fran said.

Katie took the small yellow pill from Natalie's hand, swallowed and laid her head back onto the pillow. "I'll finish the paperwork in a second."

She signed the papers and gave them to Fran a few minutes later. "I'll be okay now. You go back to work, Natalie."

"I'll be back about five-thirty. You're coming home with me tonight."

Fran spun around. "Oh, I don't know if that's wise."

"Tomorrow's Saturday. I won't leave her side," Natalie promised.

"Well, don't, because you never know how they're going to react when the restraining order is delivered."

The next morning Natalie insisted that Katie go to Barrington Hospital after leaving the shelter to get X-rays and an examination of her wounds. "No broken bones but you're lucky considering the extent of your bruises. You could have been injured a lot worse. You're going to be sore and hurting for several days," the doctor said and then wrote her a prescription for pain. Then the doctor made a record of the assault, took photos and warned Katie to heed the restraining order.

Knowing the restraining order had been delivered that morning Katie waited all day to be immersed in remorse of some kind, but couldn't seem to summon the energy for it. That evening she felt surprisingly calm while enjoying Natalie's delicious spaghetti dinner, her first real food in two days. "I have to speak with Martha and Tommy and Mathew as soon as possible," she told Natalie. "I don't know what Jeff has told them."

"I think you should call the kids when Jeff's not there," Natalie said. "You don't have to talk to Jeff." She picked up her wine glass from the table. "Now, or ever, if you don't want to."

"I apologize for unloading my horror stories on you all day," Katie said. "But thank you for listening. It's a tremendous relief to be honest with you, finally."

"Wish you had earlier, girl. A wonder you haven't gotten whiplash adjusting to that heaven and hell relationship."

"You know what? At the shelter I kept imagining my mom and sister Marijo and I together at Mom's kitchen table, like old times. Then today I wondered if I could talk Marijo into meeting me in Minnesota. Maybe I could start to heal my soul while eating my mom's vanilla cupcakes with chocolate sauce and whipped cream. Now that's really nuts. I swore when I left home, I'd never eat another of those desserts in my lifetime. We had those cupcakes every single Sunday." She paused and took a drink of ice water. "I want to talk to my mother, but I don't know how much I can tell her. Damn! I feel so rootless. Maybe sleeping in my childhood bed is just what I need."

"Why not go? We'll manage at the paper."

"I might," Katie said realizing that her entire body suddenly felt like a rubber band gone slack. "Yeah, I think I'm going to do it."

Natalie pushed her chair back. "I'll make us an Irish coffee. We both deserve to relax a little. We've earned that."

"Enough about *my* screwed up life," Katie said. "Tell me the latest about you and your handsome Nathan in New York."

"We're still tight," Natalie said. "Last weekend he said he might look into teaching at the University of Rhode Island."

"Well. So how does that strike you?"

Natalie smiled. "I told him, 'That would be interesting' because I wanted you and Steve to get to know him and he laughed."

She got up and went to the kitchen. A few minutes later she brought two glasses of Irish coffee with a dab of Cool Whip on top back to the table and sat down. "I don't know if I'm too stuck in my ways to have somebody around all the time. We have a good arrangement now. Energy-packed weekends in New York, romantic as hell, and then we stay out of each other's hair the rest of the week. Don't know if I want to spoil that."

Katie took a sip of Irish coffee and laughed. "You don't know how beautiful romantic weekends and free the rest of the week sounds to me about now."

"Glad to see you smile again," Natalie said. "Try to keep doing it."

Katie decided to speak to Jeff when he called the next morning although the sound of his voice made her squeeze the receiver with both hands to steady herself.

"I figured you'd be at Natalie's. Okay, Katie, come home. We have to straighten this out." He was using his fatherly tone that Katie despised. "I told Mrs. Lewis to take a few days off so we'll have some privacy."

"Get a therapist, Jeff," Katie said just from habit. Her old mantra sounded weary now, lacking any conviction. "Or do you still believe you don't need one?"

"Don't start that again."

"Look, I have to get away for a while. I'm going to Minnesota." She might as well tell him; he would make the kids tell him where she was anyway.

"Your mother doesn't have to know our business," he sputtered. "If you'd been at the airport instead of at your dinner party, all would be fine now."

"Media Women's Association meeting, Jeff. It's a professional organization. I'm their chairperson now." Let him think it was a conspiracy, a whole organization of women out to get him. She clamped her fingers tighter to the phone. "Nothing gives you the right to assault me. Nothing!"

"Assault? Spouting legalese now? It's that butch attorney speaking, not you. What the hell are you trying to do to me with a restraining order? Nobody can tell me what to do in my own home. Don't forget that!"

But was that fear in his voice? "Our home, Jeff. I could tell you to move out if I wanted to," she said.

"Don't talk stupid. You should have guessed how I'd react to having to wait at the airport the other night."

"You bastard!" she snapped back propelled by months of stored up anger that was searing her brain that second. "Stop making excuses for yourself." She took in some air. *He doesn't care. He doesn't care about what he did to me.* "You tripped me and hit me in the face. I fell. I got hurt. You shithead!"

She glanced up at Natalie who had come back into the room. "I'm going to tell you one thing and hang up," Katie said. "I'm coming to the house tomorrow afternoon to get clothes for my trip. My attorney has forbidden you by court order from being there. And I'll have a court appointed security officer with me."

"You bet, princess."

She replaced the phone and tossed her head back letting her small victory warm her. How long had it been since she had spoken this freely to Jeff about anything?

Fran Marconi had instructed the police officer to follow Katie to the house, wait outside and follow her back to Natalie's. This was fine with Katie; she didn't want to be there a minute longer than necessary. Even with the officer standing guard at the front driveway she wouldn't relax until she was on the road back to Natalie's. She'd already stuffed handfuls of lingerie, cosmetics and a hair dryer into one suitcase when she reached for an empty suitcase on the floor. But she was shocked when she straightened up and found Jeff staring back at her from the open bedroom doorway.

"Get out of here! Now!" she shouted.

"Running home to your Norman Rockwell family? Going to tell your troubles to your mommy and sister and those Eagle Scout brothers of yours? Especially that oldest one. A regular Captain Marvel, that one, according to you. Sure, you think you can just up and leave me with Martha and Mathew and Tommy. What do you care about us?"

Katie looped her fingers into the handle of the already packed suitcase. "I'm leaving now. Get out of my way."

He dug his fingers into her arm. "Don't go, Katie. Remember that first summer you came here?"

"Move, Jeff."

He stepped forward, shoulders hunched. "You can't just waltz out of here like you haven't a damn care in the world."

"Yes I can. You're the one breaking the law by being here."

"Breaking the law? In my own home?"

He slid towards her, spidery cheek veins rising to the surface, red blotches forming on his forehead. "You're getting rotten advice from that mouthy lawyer of yours. She doesn't tell me what I can do."

"No? Look at the bruises on me. I could have you arrested this very minute. Get out of my way! I'm leaving. There's a court ordered officer waiting for me out front. Didn't you see him?"

"Yeah. I saw him. Which is why I parked up the road and tracked through the woods to the back door." He grabbed the packed case from her hand, snapped it open and dumped the contents onto the floor. Then he lunged toward her, wrapping his hands around her back.

"Don't," she screamed. Dropping to the floor, out of his grasp, she tried to crawl toward the door.

He jumped in front of her, swung her to her feet and pulled her up to his chest. "You can't go." Crooking his head to the side, he smiled. "Those people are confusing you, Katie. You know you love me."

From the inside of her mouth that felt like sawdust she yelled, "Let go of me! Let go!"

Yanking her closer to him, he slapped both arms around her back. "You're just upset. Let me help you...."

"You help me? You selfish idiot!" she yelled.

Smacking a hand over her mouth, he growled, "Shut up. Martha's in the wing. She'll hear your shrieking."

Katie bent her leg and shoved her knee hard into his groin. "Get your hands off me!"

He groaned. With his complexion fiery red now, he gripped her throat with both hands and dug his fingers into her neck. "I want you to listen to me. I know you could be a good wife if you tried."

Pushing his chin hard with the ball of her hand, she loosened his grip on her throat, got a breath and screamed, "Martha! Martha! Get the officer!"

Jeff tightened his hands around her neck again until he heard the back door opening. He jerked away from Katie. "Stupid bitch!" he groaned before running from the room. He pushed past Martha on the stairs and dashed toward the back door.

Katie fell to the bed as Martha bolted up the rest of the stairs and into the bedroom.

Out of breath, Martha plopped next to Katie on the bed. "I was on the back steps. I heard you scream."

"He wouldn't have let go of me if he hadn't heard you coming," Katie said. Still trembling, her body couldn't seem to believe the danger was over.

Martha grabbed Katie's hand. "How did he get in?"

With adrenalin still pumping through her veins, Katie heard the young security officer sprinting up the stairs and calling out, "Mrs. O'Connell! I saw someone running at the side of the house toward the woods. Are you all right?"

"My husband," she said. "He's gone. Just wait for me. I'll be down in a few minutes."

"I'm sorry. I chased him, but I lost him. I never saw him enter the house. You have to get out of here. Do you want to charge him?"

"I'm leaving town in two days. For now, I just want to get back to my friend's cottage."

"I'll wait at the bottom of the stairs and follow you there."

"Yes. Go back to Natalie's," Martha said. "This is so bad. He's my father, but..."

Katie wrapped an arm around Martha's shoulder. "Come with me to Minnesota," she said.

"Nah. I'll be okay. I'll walk over to my friend Melissa's and stay there for a couple of hours until Mat and Tommy come home."

"Please come with me," Katie begged.

"Never mind me. My dad won't hurt *me*." Martha's face had drained of color. "You have to go now! The officer is waiting. Sure you can you drive? Or should you ride with the officer?"

"I'll drive. Give me another minute."

Katie held Martha's hand. "I'm sorry. You're too young for this. This isn't how love should end up, Martha."

Martha shook her head. "I don't understand why he's so angry. You loved him." She paused and Katie hoped for once that Martha would give way to tears. Instead, she whispered, "But then, so did my mother. And what good did that do her?"

"I think it's time we stop trying to figure him out, Martha. We have to take care of ourselves now. Please, please come to Minnesota with me."

"He'd probably send the FBI after us."

"I'll take that chance if you want to come." Katie stood up. "I think I've stopped shaking."

Martha picked up Katie's belongings from the floor and stuffed them back into the empty case. The officer met them at the front door, ushered them down the path and waited for Katie in his police car.

Martha leaned into the car window; Katie kissed her on the cheek and then watched her back away. Tall for her age, a mass of Raphael-like blonde hair framing her high cheekbones, her wide blue eyes defiant as ever, Martha stood still on the path. Katie felt powerless knowing she had no legal authority over the girl. Nor the boys.

"I'll call you when I get to Minnesota," Katie called out. "Sure you won't come?"

Throwing both arms in the air, Martha waved back. "You know me. I'll be fine," she said.

Oh, sure you will. With a lot of help from the Almighty, Katie prayed, allowing herself a last look back at this house of despair.

Chapter Ten

With her suitcase tucked into a closet in the third floor bedroom that had been hers and Marijo's, Katie went into the bathroom to examine her bruises – almost at the blue stage but starting to fade. She touched up the patch of make-up on her cheek bruise, retied the silk scarf around her neck hiding the finger marks at her throat and went downstairs.

She sat down at the dining table and waited for her mother to join her. This old table brought back so many memories for Katie. Every Sunday she and Marijo would lay out the family's rosebud china on a lace cloth that had once won their mother a first prize at an August county fair. All one winter, their mom had sat rim-rod in a high-backed rocker in the front parlor, her crochet needles clicking effortlessly while she listened to her favorite crooners, Bing Crosby, Frankie Lane and Frank Sinatra on the radio. That spring, she threw the wheat colored lace cloth across the back of the sofa. "Well, what do you think?" she had asked, chin out, eyes waiting for approval.

"A gold medal winner if ever I saw one," Katie had exclaimed.

Katie recalled now how that tablecloth covering scratches on this old mahogany table had seemed to cast a mysterious spell over her mother, auburn hair tucked behind her ears, curly wisps framing her face as steam rising up from hot vegetables misted her cheeks, enhancing her brunette beauty,

Katie and Marijo would carry the pot roast, gravy, potatoes, green beans and carrots from the gas range in the kitchen to the dining table as their oldest brother John pulled back a chair for their mom at one end of the table. John and Katie sat on one side, Marijo and the younger brothers Dennis and James on the other side and their father presided at the head of the table.

Like clockwork, when their father finished the last of his meal he leaned back in his armchair and asked, "Molly, are we having vanilla cupcakes with chocolate sauce and whipped cream for dessert?"

Every week he asked, and every week his wife answered, "Yes, Arthur."

Katie had understood early on that her father held the key to her mother's happiness. He had the power to put a smile on her lips or to drain the color from her cheeks in the space of one minute. Her mother tried many times to explain this phenomenon to Katie by hunching up her shoulders and declaring: "Men, can't live with them, can't live without them. And can't please them either."

Back then, Katie and her mother chatted constantly when they were alone, which was often once Marijo and the boys were involved in high school activities. Scouring dishes in hot water with Ivory soap at the kitchen sink, or hanging dripping wet shirts on a rope clothesline in the basement, Katie and her mom gossiped about anything – family, the neighborhood, the world. Yet, at the moment, Katie had no idea how to tell her mother about her current troubles. On the phone from Rhode Island she'd simply presented her mother with a rosy picture of her new life.

Her mother, bustling into the room carrying a coffee pot and cookies on a tray, interrupted Katie's recollections. She poured the freshly brewed coffee into their cups while examining Katie more thoroughly, then slid into a chair across from her daughter. "Is everything okay with you, honey?" she asked. "I was afraid to ask on the way home from the airport.

Always in the past, you've given me more than a two-day notice that you were coming."

Katie poured cream into her coffee and looked up at her mom. "Jeff and I are going through a terrible time," she said.

Molly reached over to give her daughter's hand a gentle tap. "There isn't a couple alive that hasn't had their share of rough times, dear."

Katie wanted her mother to hear her out, wanted to tell her this was really bad, worse than a rough time, but her mother continued to give her encouragement. "Things seem worse at the time than they do later," she said. "People mend hard feelings and go on." She passed a plate of cookies to her daughter. "Peanut butter. I made them special for you. I know you love them."

Katie bit into a warm cookie while noticing the wispy brown curls, streaked with gray now that still framed her mother's face. "Whatever happened, you'll get through it," her mother insisted. "When you decide to do something, there's no stopping you. Never was. Taking off for the west coast at eighteen! How I fretted over you, at the same time bragging about you to everyone. A wonder my friends didn't crown me." She took a drink of her coffee. "Nothing gets my Katie down for long."

Picking up another cookie, savoring the taste of melting peanut butter and brown sugar on her tongue, Katie longed for the time when she believed in such simple solutions. "That used to be true, Mom," she said.

Her mother reached across the table and patted her hand. "I'm sure it's still true. Don't you think you two can come to an understanding? When Jeff came to visit with you for a few days that time, everyone thought you had married a prince."

"He can be very charming," Katie said while restirring the cream in her coffee. "Were you truly happy with our dad?" she asked, hoping to re-start their conversation from another direction.

"Happy? I'm not sure how to measure happiness. I loved him. Admired him for sure. He was so intelligent. Always preoccupied, though, you know how he was. For the first few years I made myself miserable. Why can't he appreciate me more? Why can't he be more talkative? Then I came to terms. He wasn't one to go around showing off his emotions or conversing a lot. And that was that." She held her wedding ring out in front of her and smiled as though her husband had just slipped it on her finger. "I had women friends to cut up with during the day. And to talk to when I was blue. So I made out. Florence Olsen and I have cried into our coffee cups together many a time."

"But you knew he loved you?"

"Well, yes. When he worked late, though, I sometimes questioned if he knew I was there except to pull his supper out of the oven when he got home. I didn't stew about it, though, not after I decided to take him as he was. What man wants a sourpuss wife around all the time?" She nudged Katie's arm. "Men don't always show their love the way we want them to."

Katie looked hard at her mother but then stopped herself from saying what she'd come home to tell her. Her thoughts had diverted to her father. Why couldn't he have shown his love in the simple ways his wife wanted? Was that asking too much? Katie didn't think so, but she saw in her mother's eyes that she'd made peace with her memories. Let it alone, she told herself. "I'm sure he loved you very much, Mom," she said.

"Oh, yes. Of course he did." She reached for Katie's hand again. "I've missed him every minute of these past four years since he passed." She went silent for a moment. "You don't have to tell me what happened between you and Jeff if you don't want to. Just try to get to the bottom of the problem, honey. A marriage is a precious thing." She passed the cookie plate to Katie again and smiled. "I never taught you to be a quitter, did I?"

The next day after picking up Marijo at the small connector airport outside of Minona, all three women decided for old time's sake to stop at an old high school hangout on Main Street. Katie glanced around Carlson's Ice Cream Parlor with its marble top tables and its candy displays inside pane glass cabinets while enjoying the familiar sweet frosty air.

Patting the blonde bouffant hairdo she'd worn for the past six or seven years and brandishing a smile she'd perfected as a high school cheerleader, Marijo told their teenage waitress, "I'll have a cherry chocolate Coke, please."

"A what?" the girl asked.

"Just write it down," their mother, Molly Symth, said, then pointed to herself and Katie. "And we'll each have a hot fudge sundae." Shrugging her shoulders, the girl wandered back to the soda fountain.

"Maybe they no longer make cherry chocolate Cokes?" Katie wondered out loud.

"Oh, they will, or I'll march into the back room and have a talk with Ben Carlson myself," Molly said. Leaning forward to share a confidence with her daughters, she whispered, "It's been forty some years since I worked in this place. Still crisp and clean though, isn't it?" She cocked her head toward the waitress. "Everything the same except those low cut jeans and that tight sweater on our waitress. We had to wear uniforms. Black dresses and white half aprons. And a little lace tiara pinned to the top of our heads." Molly gazed off into another time. "I thought I was the cat's meow."

"The cat's meow, Mom?" Katie nudged Marijo. "Is that like hot shit?"

"Katie!" Molly's mouth curled up slightly at the corners. "Well, I guess I was hot shit, all right."

Katie roared but Marijo covered her eyes and shook her head at both of them. "You're nasty, nasty as ever," Marijo scolded Katie, sending Katie into a fit of giggles. Since Marijo's arrival at Minona Airport all three had slid easily into roles from their past.

Katie glanced around the ice cream parlor again, then back at Marijo and her mother. Her mother was proud of her, always had been. She had encouraged Katie to follow her dreams, while waiting on her own husband hand and foot. The fact was, Katie didn't know how her mother would react to the truth about Jeff. With anger for certain, but also with sadness she was sure, and the thought of letting her mother down that much was starting to make her feel ill. God, how she hated to disappoint the people who loved her.

Molly answered her phone after dinner that evening: "Oh, Jeff. You too," she said. "Nice talking with you too...I'm fine...Yes, we're enjoying the visit...it's a long time since I've had both of my girls to myself. Katie says she's going to take the call up in her bedroom. Yes, same to you...Next time, come in the summer. It's beautiful then...Wait a minute, now."

Sinking onto the old patchwork quilt on her bed, Katie reached for the phone on a stand between her bed and Marijo's bed. "Hi, Katie," Jeff said. Since Katie had arrived she'd been visualizing the captain's house only in shades of gray, never in color. Her mental picture of Jeff now had him sitting in their darkened bedroom. "How's the visit going?" he asked.

She braced herself: Oh, God, is he going to be chatty? "The visit has been good for me. I've done a lot of thinking," she said.

"Me too." He paused. "The kids are okay. Martha says she's spoken with you a few times. We need you, Katie."

"Don't start, Jeff," she said. "Not from a thousand miles away. I'm coming back next week." Just as well to tell him; he'd find out anyway.

"Fine. Give me your arrival time. I'll meet the plane." He'd come alive, his tone changing, voice suddenly charged. Had he convinced himself she'd been off on a short vacation, visiting Minnesota, the winter wonderland of her youth? How he could pretend! And how he'd like her to do the same.

Although the restraining order was still in effect, she decided to take a chance on meeting him in a safe public place. "I'm taking the Minoma connector plane to Milwuakee, United to Boston and Seacoast to Barrington on Friday. Arriving at 8:00 p.m. We need to talk."

"A good arrival time. Excellent. We can go out to dinner from the airport."

She pulled at the scarf at her neck. "No. No dinner."

"We'll have to have dinner. We might as well..."

"No plans, Jeff. I'll see you at the airport."

As Katie hung up Marijo poked her head into the bedroom. "Is Jeff missing you?" she asked.

"I suppose so. In his own way." Katie thought about speaking the words now that would drain blood from her sister's face, extinguish her smile, tear up her eyes and alter the secure age old contract between them. The one that promised Katie would be the carefree adventure seeking daughter and that Marijo would admire that in Katie while at the same time enjoying her own predictable, blissful life with her decent guy husband and three beautiful kids.

But before Katie could begin her confession to her sister, Marijo smiled looking relieved. "Well that makes me feel better. Since I arrived I felt you were holding something back. I don't know what, but something. You deserve to be happy, honey. I'm glad you and Jeff are okay in spite of all those kids that landed on you. These men can be hopeless, can't they?"

she said. "Let him miss you. He'll appreciate you more when you return. God knows what I'll find when I get home. As long as Sam has gotten the kids off to school, I don't really care. It's worth it for you and me to have a visit like this."

Katie had meant to be honest but her earlier desire to confide in either her mother or sister seemed less pressing.

"Yes, it's been forever since we've set aside time for us."

Marijo flopped onto her twin bed. "Just like old times. You know I've always envied you, little sister. Mom loves us all, but you're the one she brags about. She's always lived vicariously through you. I know that. I guess I have too."

"Don't. You have no reason. You have so much." But Katie left it there. Really, why ruin this priceless visit by laying her gloom on her mother and her sister. Besides, just being reunited with them had managed to lift her mood. "Let's join Mom in the kitchen. I smell the coffee perking, don't you?" Katie said.

As the wing of the plane dipped and circled before landing, Katie had a view out her window of the coastline and Barrington, Rhode Island nestled between two long fingers of rocks and sand. It was there, after all – Jeff, the captain's house, Jeff's boat, his airplane, the yacht club, the *Gazette*, the Catch of the Day Tavern, the shelter. In Minnesota, she'd had a silly dream one night that it had all disappeared like Brigadoon and then she had awakened and glanced around her childhood room and thought good, I have a hundred years to decide what to do.

The eight-passenger plane came to a stop on the runway and she saw Jeff standing alone by the gate. Gusts of chilly evening wind sweeping across the airfield had most likely sent others inside. But not Jeff; he leaned on the metal fence holding his down jacket together at the neck, and for one short moment, Katie wanted everything to be different, to hurry down the stairs, rush over to him and throw herself into his arms.

She turned her head to the side when she reached the small terminal building forcing his kiss to brush across her cheek. "Let's get some coffee inside while I wait for my bags."

He threw his arm around her shoulder. "Two coffees," he told the waitress at the lunch counter as they sat down. His cheeks glowed pink from the cold. "I have a proposition," he said. "You know the trip to Spain we've planned for so long? How would you like to go next week?"

Katie's hand moved involuntarily to the neck of her turtleneck sweater where she kept it. "I have to tell you something, Jeff."

His smile barely faded. "Let bygones be bygones," he said. "I want to start at square one. I'm willing to do things differently if you are. I have a lot of ideas..."

She was glad to be sitting down considering what she was going to say. "I don't see how I could love you again after this. And I am sure something awful would happen if we were to try to stay together. Get help for yourself, Jeff."

"Nothing terrible will happen. We're both worn out. We need to get away. We can take two weeks instead of one in Spain." He touched one of her hands. "We'll make up for lost time."

She slid her hand away from him and wrapped both hands around her hot coffee mug, her mother's voice echoing in her ear. "Men don't always show their love the way we want them to. Better to take them as they are." But during the flight back, somewhere over Michigan or Vermont, it had occurred to Katie that she'd been doing exactly that for months. Still clutching her coffee mug, she turned back to Jeff. "You say you love me, Jeff, but you don't act as if you do. And you'll never change without professional help."

"Don't mention that subject again, Katie. Therapy's not for me. I realize that now."

"Look at me." She twisted all the way around on the stool to face him directly. "I don't think you get what's happening. I could have had you arrested before I left for Minnesota. I shouldn't even be speaking to you now. The restraining order is still in effect."

"Don't threaten me, Katie," he growled through bared teeth. "You can't control me with ultimatums."

Control him? When had he last followed through on anything she'd asked for? During the past ten days, she'd been seeing his violence in a brand new way. In the past she'd treated his fits like crises of the moment, when in reality, they were a way of life with him, just a means of getting what *he* wanted.

With raised eyebrows and thin lips, he said, "I mean it, Katie. Come with me to the car. We're going home to start over. Look at yourself. Look at what you've become. You're acting like a victim and a martyr. What's worse, I think you're enjoying it."

"Martyr, Jeff? You nearly choked me to death a week ago. Oh, hell. You may be right about what I've become. But you're dead wrong about my enjoying it." She looked into his violet blue eyes and said, "You don't get it, Jeff. I can't live with you anymore!"

Chapter Eleven

Natalie greeted Katie at the door of her cottage and grabbed her suitcase. "You're looking better," she said.

"That's not saying much, is it?" Katie smiled and slumped into a chair. "Don't know where I'll go from here but thanks for taking me in on an emergency basis again."

"Did you leave poor Jeff at the airport?"

"Yes. With a stunned look on his face."

"Good. I'll fix us some tea and get you settled in the other bedroom."

The next day Katie pulled her feet up under her in a velvet wingback chair in Natalie's living room. Alone and cradled in its immense arms, she felt as if she'd just leapt from a moving boxcar and landed on a soft bed of Kansas hay. Suddenly she wanted to call Maxine, only to tell her the truth this time. If she had been honest with Maxine in the past her friend would have come to rescue her on the next plane out of San Francisco. As the ringing started, Katie envisioned Maxine at her desk at Berkeley Women's Central surrounded by stacks of file folders, perhaps shoving an unfinished wheat germ and Feta cheese sandwich aside to answer.

Katie paused before speaking, aware that she couldn't retract anything she might tell Maxine now. Considering Katie's feminist views, Maxine had every right to think her a hypocrite for having stayed with Jeff this long. Katie's only defense would be to claim *that at least* she had *tried* to demand equality in her marriage, tried and tried, strategy after strategy.

On hearing Maxine's voice, Katie spoke quickly before changing her mind. "I haven't been truthful with you, Maxine," she began and then let the rest spill out.

"Fuck him!" Maxine yelled when Katie had finished. "Jesus, are you all right?"

"I guess. Except for knowing I've screwed up royally."

"You didn't know he'd be like this. He seemed a little shifty to me, but no way would I have suspected he was a potential abuser. Shoot, I'm not that brilliant. You're the last person I would imagine this happening to. Well, that's stupid. It could happen to any of us."

"I've wanted to tell you from the beginning."

"Why didn't you? I'm furious with you."

"I don't know."

She heard Maxine suck in a breath. "Don't let him near you! I'm going to call every couple of days. Give me Natalie's phone number. And call me if you feel you are weakening or even considering going back to him."

When Katie hung up the phone an unexpected vision of Jeff and her in love and holding hands in San Francisco drifted before her. Mocking her, she thought, quickly shaking herself loose from it. For the time being, she would have to hold herself together with safety pins and glue and Scotch tape if necessary.

On Monday evening Katie spotted Jeff waiting alongside her car in the *Gazette* parking lot as she left the building. She rushed over to her car and around to the driver's side but he caught her by the arm. "Don't do this, Katie," he said.

"Let go or I'll scream. Someone will come." She searched wildly about the lot and in front of the back exit where other employees were starting to leave the building.

Seeing them, Jeff dropped her arm, swiped a palm across his forehead and skulked away. Over his shoulder, he said, "I know you're staying with Natalie."

She got into her car and grabbed the steering wheel with both hands but all that weekend, like the needle of a compass whirling 360 degrees nonstop, she seemed to lose all sense of direction. But there was no time for indecision now with Jeff stalking her. She couldn't put Natalie or herself in that kind of danger. She would have to tell Fran Marconi to proceed with a legal separation at once. *But what about his kids* she worried immediately. Mathew would start college next fall; Tommy would finish high school in two years, but Martha wouldn't be going away to a prep school for three years. Maybe the school would let Martha start a year early, she hoped. Katie took a deep breath. "Slow down. One thing at a time," she told herself.

Katie called Martha when she reached Natalie's cottage and was glad the girl had answered in the children's wing. "Martha, I know you're worried, honey. I want you to know what's happening. Do you think you and Mathew and Tommy could meet me somewhere to talk?"

"Yes. We all want to know what happened Friday when you came back from Minnesota. Before you returned, Dad said you were coming back here to live with us. But I couldn't believe that was true. He's going to be in New York tomorrow night. Can we see you then?"

"Great. I'll pick you up at home about five-thirty."

They filed into the Chili Pepper as though nothing had changed since the last time they were there. But everything had changed and they all knew it. "Let's grab our usual corner booth," Martha said leading them through the restaurant.

"Mathew, why don't you put in our usual orders?" Katie said.

With their food finally spread out on the table, Tommy asked, "Are you coming back, Katie?"

All three turned to Katie and waited. "I can't, Tommy. I'm sure Martha's told you the reason I left that night and also what happened at the house when I came back to get some clothes. I can't put myself through that ever again. I don't think I could help any of you now if I *did* come back."

"You told us you wouldn't leave," Tommy said. "I get what you're saying now but you stayed before when Dad took all his mentals. So I didn't know."

"But this time he hurt me. He chased me. I fell. I bruised my face and my leg and my hip. At the house two days later he grabbed my throat and tried to choke me. I don't know what would have happened if Martha hadn't heard me scream."

Tommy looked away from Katie and down at his plate. He picked up his burrito and took a small bite.

"I want you all to know that part of the reason I've stayed this long has been for you guys. I don't want to put you through any more traumas, but..."

Finally Mathew spoke. "None of us blames you. But it's going to be tough. I feel exactly like the day my mom told my dad she couldn't stand to be afraid every day any longer. And then he took off."

"Damn!" Katie said. "This is what I dreaded. All of you being hurt again."

Martha narrowed her eyes at her brothers. "If you ask me, you two are acting like babies. We're safe and sound. And Mrs. Lewis is there all day now."

"Yeah, bossing us around," Tommy said.

Katie drew back her shoulders hoping to convey an assurance she certainly didn't feel. "How is your dad acting?

Please tell me he's not turning on any of you. He's never done that."

"He's seems rattled with trying to keep order on the home front," Mathew said. "But he hasn't blown a gasket yet." He shook his head. "I asked him if we should go back to living with Mom, but he said, "No way. You will all finish school here. Period."

Katie wished she could say something brilliant to help them but nothing came to mind. Instead she swallowed hard and tried to control her rage that this cruel injustice should be foisted on these kids again. Her voice came out wet and blubbery in spite of her efforts to convey confidence. "I'm so sorry about all of this," she said.

"We can keep going to therapy," Martha offered. "I'll go."

Katie forced a smile. "Sure, let's try to work that out. It would be a help to all of us. I'll call Dr. Henry."

"I'm in," Mathew said.

"And you, Tommy?" Katie asked.

"I guess," he answered, chin resting on his chest.

Mathew rewrapped his taco. "I'll eat this later."

Tommy slapped a napkin over his half eaten burrito. "I'm not hungry now, either."

"I'm here for you," Katie said, thinking *what an empty promise that is: how could I possibly be there for them now?*

"I wish I knew what I could have done differently," she said. "We'll just have to figure things out now as we go. Any of you can call me at work or at Natalie's any time."

They got up and left the restaurant. Before getting in the car, Martha nudged Katie and nodded toward her brothers, "I'll keep an eye on them for you. And Dad too."

Jeff tried to leave a message for Katie on Natalie's voice mail the following evening when he returned from New York, but dissolved in tears and hung up before finishing. "I can't fix you, Jeff," Katie whispered to the machine and then pressed the erase button. "I've tried everything, caresses, sweet words, letting you have your way. Nothing has worked."

Every cell of her body wanted to flee Rhode Island and escape back to California, but Fran had advised her to stay for the next six or seven months and see herself through the legal process or lose more in every way than she already had lost.

Having gone three weeks without hearing from Jeff, Katie started to relax. She had intended to get her own place immediately but Natalie asked her to stay on with her as long as she wished. "After the divorce, you can make real decisions for yourself," Natalie said.

"I'm actually relieved not to have to uproot myself this minute," Katie admitted while insisting she pay half of their monthly expenses from here on.

A month later she heard from Jeff again. This time he called her at the office. "I had my first session with a therapist yesterday," he said in a calm voice considering the state he'd been in the last time he'd tried to leave a message.

Swiveling her chair around to face the wall, Katie pressed the phone to her ear. "I'm glad for you." Recalling his past resistance to therapy and references to shrinks and quacks and witch doctors, however, her doubts sprang into action at once. "How did you locate him?"

"Through the AMA. He's a psychiatrist."

"A psychiatrist. Good."

"Dr. Louis Sherman. He's in Martinsville, half an hour south. I gave him permission to talk with you if you want to call him."

"I don't think I can do that," Katie said. "It would be too difficult."

"Then would it be all right to call you about my progress from time to time?"

She fidgeted with the phone cord. "I suppose so. Just leave your report on Natalie's voice mail." When she hung up she felt a little like a child being lured into a dark forest by an enchanted flute. *Oh, well,* she told herself, *I can always erase the messages before listening to them.*

That evening, Katie felt disoriented as she got out of her car in the Catch Tavern parking lot. A bit like a dolphin released to the sea before it was ready, she decided. Even the sight of Steve coming to meet her was of little comfort. "Hey, girl," he said taking her hand. "About time you joined the human race again."

She slipped into his booth across from him. "Where's Natalie?" she asked.

Steve gestured toward a group seated at a table near the bar. "Being sociable. It's a crisp night. How about an Irish coffee to warm you?"

"Thanks. That sounds great." She glanced around the room. "Busy place tonight."

He ordered an Irish coffee and another beer from the waitress and turned back to Katie. "It's country music night. The Rhode Island chaps are all cowboys tonight. Those sorry friends of mine at the bar too."

"I'll bet if you asked those sorry friends they would do anything for you."

Steve smiled, his dark eyes crinkling at the corners. "And would that include you?"

"Of course," she responded, pleased that this was an answer she couldn't have given him two months ago when immersed in life with Jeff and the kids.

Steve accepted the Irish coffee and beer from the waitress and then asked, "How are you doing, Katie? I mean really."

She dropped her coat from her shoulders to the bench and looked across at Steve, casual in his turtleneck cable sweater, his face open and accessible as usual. "Sometimes good, sometimes not at all good." She paused. "Maybe I'm losing it, Steve."

"I expect you've been through plenty. Go easy on yourself."

She ran her fingers nervously through her long auburn hair. "Has Natalie told you why I left Jeff?" Moving into dangerous territory and unsure of the terrain, she let go of her hair and wondered: *how much am I willing to tell Steve?*

"Of course, I knew something horrendous must have happened when you flew to Minnesota without notice and then moved in with Natalie. Natalie didn't offer me an explanation. I thought I'd let you tell me if you wanted to."

"I'm afraid of Jeff. He has a violent temper." There it was, the eight hundred pound gorilla in the middle of their table.

"You mean he's physically attacked you?"

Their eyes met and Steve reached across the table for her hand. "Yes," she answered.

He clasped both of his hands around hers. "Jesus!! Why didn't you tell me? I could have helped."

"I hadn't told anyone until I told Natalie a few days before flying to Minnesota."

"I'm not 'anyone'. How could you work on that battered women series without confiding in me?" He caressed her hand. "You're too brave for your own damn good."

She squirmed in her seat, seeing nothing courageous about any of her actions. "He's going to a psychiatrist," she said to break the tension, realizing at once the irrelevance of this information to Steve.

"Well, good for him. A little late for that, isn't it?" Looking both angry and distressed, Steve swept one hand across his forehead. "It's incomprehensible to me how a man can strike a woman."

"Do you think someone with a horrible temper can ever change?" Katie asked him.

"I don't know. A man like that has to be sick. Does Jeff hate women? I think you have to despise all women to assault any woman. And that's a lot of hate." Steve patted her hand and frowned again. "You'll have to ask someone else about Jeff's chances of recovery. My opinion would be biased, to say the least." He took a quick swallow of beer, set down his glass and reached for her hand again. "How do you know he's going to a psychiatrist?"

"He's described his sessions for me on Natalie's voice mail. I didn't want to listen but I couldn't seem to stop myself. He's not informed enough about psychoanalysis to pretend."

Having struggled a long time over the decision to tell Steve the truth, she already regretted not doing it earlier. Steve was blaming Jeff, not her. God, why should blaming Jeff for Jeff's behavior seem extraordinary to her? She reached for her glass and took a drink. "I can't seem to make plans for myself, short or long range."

"You're showing up for work every day. That's pretty amazing." He paused, then looked away.

"What?" she asked him.

"Oh, nothing."

"No what?"

"I used to wonder if our relationship would be different if you were to ever stop loving Jeff." He picked up his beer and took another swallow. "I'm sorry. I didn't mean to tell you that, but since we're being honest... No ulterior motive. I know you must be deeply involved in sorting out what happened to your marriage."

"I can't forget what he's done. But, still, it's hard to tell yourself you love someone one month and expect yourself to hate the person the next. Even when you're ordering yourself to do exactly that."

His expression softening, Steve said, "I can't bear to imagine what you've been through. Keep safe now. We want you to be around for a long, long time."

Steve's caring choked her up suddenly. Swallowing hard, she said, "I can answer your earlier question if you'd like. About how our relationship would have changed if I hadn't been committed to Jeff."

"Oh?"

She leaned across the table to be heard above the band. "I think we'd be much more than good friends by now."

He leaned forward. "I'm sure we would too."

"If I weren't so utterly confused at the moment, in fact, I'd ask you to take me home with you now." She was surprised by her own candor and even a little flustered, but not sorry she'd said it.

He laughed. "In that case, let me know the second you're no longer confused, will you?"

He stood up and still holding her hand, said, "Come on, Katie. Let's try this. I used to do a pretty mean two-step."

* * * * * * *

The following week Jeff called Katie at work again, this time, to inform her that he had purchased an ocean view lot about an hour north of Barrington where he intended to build a home. "Perfect location for sailing and retirement one day," he explained.

Katie hid her surprise and said congratulations, but this news put her in a strange, melancholy mood all morning. *This would have been our dream house*, she kept thinking: *The one we discussed so often and promised ourselves to build when the kids had all left home. But why build it now, Jeff?*

For some reason that Katie didn't understand herself, she decided to phone Jeff's Dr. Louis Sherman in Martinsville. A woman answered, recognized Katie's name, and put her on hold. A moment later, Dr. Sherman picked up. "Yes, Mrs. O'Connell. Your husband said you might be calling at some point. He has given me permission to speak to you."

"Then he *is* a patient of yours?"

"Certainly. We've been working together for several weeks now."

"I hope you don't mind my calling to verify this. Naturally, I'm still interested in his welfare." She felt foolish for checking up on Jeff as if he were a delinquent child. "I wouldn't want him to misinterpret my concern, is all."

"I understand. Call again if you like," Dr. Sherman said.

That evening when Jeff called her at the cottage she picked up the home phone for the first time. "I'm glad you spoke to Dr. Sherman," he said. "You don't know how much I wish I'd gotten therapy the first time you asked me to, Katie."

"Do it for yourself now."

"I also called to ask you a favor. Say no if you can't do it. I'd like to send you some sample pictures of wood and tiles for the house to get your opinion. Tell me if I'm overstepping."

She had already made up her mind to keep a distance between herself and this new home – this home that seemed to strike at the very heart of her aborted dreams. She appreciated the irony, however, of Jeff's finally including her in his decision making when she wanted no part of it. "I don't know why my viewpoint should matter now," she said.

"Because I have no talent along those lines. And I have no one else to ask. Don't do it if it makes you uncomfortable."

"Why should it make me uncomfortable?" she said, slapping down a sponge onto Natalie's stove and shoving it hard across the surface. "Send me the brochures; I'll check items and mail them back to you."

A few days later Natalie walked over to Katie's desk just as the mail man dropped a letter into Katie's inbox. Recognizing the handwriting, Katie whisked it up immediately and tossed the envelope into her top desk drawer. Natalie, who had been following the progress of a village council story all morning, asked Katie to take over the calls from villagers voicing objections to a proposal to build a new powerboat dock. "They become environmentalists, revolted by the overcrowded harbor, the minute they get their own berths or moorings." Natalie laughed. "Instant conversion. A sense of humor helps."

She turned from Katie and bellowed into the newsroom. "Listen up, all. No more calls for me. Reroute them to Katie for now. I have to get some other work done. I'm going to interview these good folks on the village green before their six o'clock meeting. That'll be more than we want or need."

During a short lapse between phone calls, Katie lifted the envelope from her drawer, opened it and read:
Dear Katie,
I don't know why I struck out at you, the person I love.
I realize now how I intimidated you with my
temper, using it to control our lives. Well, I have total control over
my own life these days and it's worthless without you. Please let it
not be too late for us. I love you, Jeff.

Katie wished she could share this note with Natalie or Steve but she'd already presented her friends with an impossible mission. On cue, they were supposed to be understanding of her anger at Jeff, interested in his efforts to change, and when finished jumping through those hoops, stop her from doing something foolhardy now.

She stuck the letter back in her drawer just as Steve wandered up to her desk. "You look distracted. What's wrong?" he asked her.

"A note from Jeff."

Steve bent down. "You're doing so well," he said. "Don't let him upset you now."

No one, certainly not Steve, would comprehend why she'd been buoyed by reading those few words from Jeff. Steve wouldn't understand why hearing Jeff take responsibility for the first time was gratifying to her in spite of his past unforgivable actions.

Later, when Steve left the newsroom, Katie picked up the phone and called Jeff's therapist again. Only this time she made an appointment to see him.

Chapter Twelve

"Sit down, please. Jeff tells me he wants to show you how the house he's building north of Barrington is progressing," Dr. Sherman said from behind an expanse of uncluttered, polished desk. "Has he told you that?"

"No. He has asked for my help in choosing colors and materials. But go there? I'd be concerned for my safety. The last time we were alone he tried to choke me. There were many violent explosions before that." Katie fastened her eyes on Dr. Sherman with his neatly trimmed salt and pepper hair, exquisite in a gray Italian suit.

"I know he has a history of violence," Dr. Sherman said. "That's been our prime focus in therapy. At first he tried to underplay his temper, but we got past that quickly. He's serious about his desire to recover."

"And is recovery a possibility?"

"In his case, I am optimistic. He's highly motivated and ashamed of his past actions. The AMA referred him to me because I've worked with batterers for several years, in groups and in private therapy. Jeff has a way to go, but he's moving right along – becoming more introspective and expressing some surprising insights about himself. I understand that both of his parents have passed on but I would like to know as much as possible about his childhood. Since he has given me permission to speak to you, I'd welcome any information you may want to contribute regarding his growing up years."

"I gained most of my knowledge about those years during one exchange we had before purchasing our home. If you'd like me to repeat what I remember of that conversation, I can."

"Yes, please, I'd appreciate it."

Katie folded her arms and leaned back in her chair.

"Well, the conversation started one evening when Jeff plopped himself down at the kitchen table in our rented beach cottage. He and I had been having a difference of opinion for two days regarding the purchase of a house. He was smitten with a huge old captain's house. I thought it was cumbersome and would be too much responsibility to keep up.

"Jeff opened our discussion that evening by declaring how much he hated renting. 'Actually it's the landlords I hate,' he said. 'They have an unbridled power over you. Out of the blue, they can say, "Hey, my mother-in-law needs a place, afraid you'll have to vacate," or give you some other cocked-up story. And the next time you look at yourself, you're standing in the street.' Then he thumped the table with the side of his hand three or four times – which caught me off guard."

"You mean frightened you?" Dr. Sherman asked her.

"No. I wasn't yet aware of his temper. I simply said, 'I don't think landlords can evict people as easily as they used to.'

"He answered, 'You would understand better how I feel if you'd grown up the way I did.' Then he started to tell me how his family had moved from apartment to apartment when he was a child, in and out of those, two flats downstairs and two flats upstairs, duplex houses in Queens. And how his father was always sleuthing out people who'd been evicted or moved out before their leases were up, then bargaining with their landlords to offer a month's rent free for taking over the lease. 'What a bastard, he was,' Jeff said. 'He had a foreman's job at the gas and electric. He didn't have to be that frugal. What did he care how it disrupted our lives?'

"'But the moving must have been hard on him too,' I said.

"'No, my mother did all the packing and unpacking,' Jeff answered. 'When the moving truck had unloaded our stuff, my father crawled into his own bed in a new flat in a new neighborhood that looked like the old one to him, row houses, wide sidewalks, trees sprouting up out of the cement every so often. My mother's bridge club, her butcher and green grocer were all back in the old neighborhood. What did he care?'"

"But you believed his account of this constant moving?" Dr. Sherman asked while bending over his desk to write on a notepad.

"Oh, yes, I believed him because he was getting flushed and upset as he always did when mentioning his father. I was not convinced though that he was telling me *everything* about his father.

"'What about you?' I asked him. 'How bad did you feel about being the new kid on the block every year?'

"'Me?' he questioned, hunching up his shoulders. 'Another school. Another principal. New teacher. New rules. I learned to adapt. By the second or third move, I had it down to a science.' Then I remember he shoved a flat palm across the air in front of his face as if he were performing a one-handed butterfly stroke and said, 'I could feel out a situation, just like that. Sitting on our stoop, I studied the kids horsing around on the street. I'd try to figure out which one was boss. You could tell by the way the other guys tilted their heads when he spoke and how they laughed hardest at his jokes. Within a week or so I knew what I had to do to fit in. There's always something a particular person or group is missing. The secret is discovering what it is, then figuring out how to provide it for them.'

"Doctor, I let him talk on without interrupting because it was so rare for him to divulge anything about his early life."

Dr. Sherman nodded and motioned for Katie to continue.

"Then Jeff told me that the first time he tried this strategy he was only in the fifth grade. 'I leaned on a lamppost examining a group of kids playing kick the can across the street in our new neighborhoods,' he said. 'They were excited about another kid at school who had a terrific baseball card collection. So I sauntered up to them and mentioned casually that I had a dynamite collection myself. I said I'd show it to them as soon as we unpacked our boxes. Then I begged money off my mother, enough to take a bus to Forest Hills and some extra besides. I rummaged through the dime store and variety store there, even an expensive hobby shop and paid for cards until my money was gone. I rubbed them in the dirt when I got home so they wouldn't look as if I'd just bought them. In a matter of days, I had impressed every kid on the block with my precious cards. After a while, it got easier. Hell, by junior high, I could get myself accepted in a school or neighborhood in a month's time.'

"Jeff looked at me then and smiled, raising his eyebrows. I guessed he was quite proud of this. 'Wow,' I said. 'Very crafty.'

"For a brief moment, Doctor, I pictured a young Jeff sitting on the front steps of their duplex taking in the mannerisms of kids across the street, probably mimicking them later when he was alone in front of his bathroom mirror. And I wanted to grasp that ten-year-old boy up in my arms and hug him and somehow make him feel safer."

Dr. Sherman scribbled on his pad again while asking Katie to go on.

"'A tough way to grow up,' I told him. 'I wouldn't blame you if you hated your father back then.'

"'Oh, I hated him all right,' Jeff answered me. 'I used to fantasize how I'd beat the shit out of him when I got big enough. No big deal. By the time I could have done it, I had lost interest in the project.'

"Jeff seemed completely unaware that he had just rolled his hand into a fist. As soon as he did this, a terrible vision flashed before me."

"You mean of his father beating him?"

"Yes. I immediately asked him outright, 'Did your father ever hit you, Jeff?'

"He threw his shoulders back and said, 'Whether he did or not doesn't matter a damn bit now. It's water over the dam.'"

"'It matters!' I insisted.

"But he ignored me and said, 'What pissed me off most was how he treated my mother. I could never forgive him for that.' Then Jeff reached for my hand and squeezed my fingers gently. 'I'm sure we all have childhood memories we'd as soon forget,' he said.

"'Well, yes,' I told him but I wasn't sure about that since I had always wanted more from my own father than he was able to give me, not less. Jeff, however, had already switched back to the topic of buying the house. 'I know I'm being a pain in the ass on this captain's house thing,' he said. 'But that house would fulfill a dream of mine.'

"To be honest, Dr. Sherman, and I don't even know if this is relevant to your purposes, the word 'dream' never entered my mind when I got down to serious thinking the next day. I couldn't empathize with Jeff's romantic notions about grand old family houses. I'd helped my mother take care of a big old house all during my childhood. I knew maintaining one of these homes that Jeff called *gracious* would be work, a lot of work. I also remembered that the air had been sucked out of me two days earlier inside that huge so called gracious house with its large added wing and a lot that was isolated, six miles from the nearest village in a wooded area off the main highway.

"Sorry, I'm rattling on here, Doctor. In the end, I sympathized with Jeff's need for his dream house and he said he'd hire housekeeping help and we bought the captain's house."

Katie waited for Dr. Sherman to finish the notes he was still scribbling furiously. Then he stood up and thanked her for her 'valuable information'. "By the way," he said, "my positive assessment of Jeff is based partly on the fact, as you must know, that he is very intelligent and a quick study, but also on his commitment to continue in prolonged treatment."

Dr. Sherman walked her to the door and then paused. "As for your meeting him at the house," he said. "First ask yourself if you want to go. If the answer is yes, set certain rules beforehand. Drive your own car of course. If you feel ill at ease, stay in your car and don't go inside the house. By all means steer the talk away from past sensitive topics."

"Do you think he is still furious with me? I certainly don't intend to place myself in jeopardy again."

"Jeff's anger is directed at himself now, not you. He is contrite. He wants to regain your respect no matter what. He stresses that constantly. You'll have to talk eventually, no matter what decision you make together about the future. Naturally, the decision whether or not to meet him there is yours."

* * * * * * *

Katie rushed back into the newsroom an hour later having already decided to keep her rendezvous with Dr. Sherman to herself for now. She sank into her chair and then noticed a note from Steve on a slip of paper pinned to her phone: "Katie, please come see me when you return."

Talking to Steve would be a nice reprieve she decided, hurrying to the other end of the newsroom.

"Hey, there," he said as she approached his desk. "How would you like to join me for dinner tonight? I need to talk to someone with two feet on the ground for a change."

Katie burst into a hearty laugh. "And you're asking me? Me? Moi? You deserve better, but nevertheless, I accept your invitation. I'll meet you at the Catch after work."

She glanced around the tavern until she saw Steve standing at the bar, but then stopped short. A tall attractive brunette woman stood next to him with her hand resting on his shoulder. Then suddenly the woman swung around to face him and placed a finger on his lips. They smiled spontaneously at one another and then laughed at what may have been an old joke they shared. Katie's first impulse was to turn and leave the restaurant but she couldn't seem to move. She knew she was being ridiculous. Steve had dated several different Rhode women and had many women friends. This, however, was the first time she had actually seen him involved in what appeared to be intimate discourse with a woman.

Finally Katie began to inch backwards toward the entrance but Steve spotted her and waved. Tossing her head casually in a gesture she hoped would designate casualness, she strolled over to the bar.

Steve reached for her hand. "Katie, I'd like you to meet an old friend of mine," he said. "Sidney, meet Katie, a colleague at the paper."

"Oh," Sidney responded with a smile. "You work together."

Steve touched Sidney's shoulder. "Not that I wouldn't enjoy the company of two fascinating women, but Katie and I have some business issues to discuss tonight."

Sidney swept two fingers down the side of Steve's cheek and quipped, "Another time then, Steve."

Steve and Katie slipped away from the bar and settled into a booth facing one another. "I think I'll order a martini for a change of pace," Steve said.

"I'll have the same," Katie said, thinking a martini might be just the help she needed to restore her composure. Seeming perfectly relaxed, Steve ordered their drinks while providing no additional information about his gorgeous earlier companion.

Katie took a sip of her cocktail while questioning her own reaction to seeing Steve in this brand new light. She had no right to jealousy, for heaven's sake, if that's what she was experiencing. Thank goodness, Steve dove straight into a lively conversation about current affairs and the state of the universe while Katie's mind had seemingly turned to mush. Finally forcing herself to take part, she offered her latest take on these solemn subjects, but at the same time was puzzled. Why did she and Steve need this special occasion to examine subjects they dissected at the paper nearly every day with their coffee?

Then, without warning Steve became introspective, switching to the subject of his own present life. He was happy, he said, but of late he'd been wondering if he was *too* satisfied. "Do you think that can happen?" he asked.

"I suppose so," Katie said. "But what's wrong with enjoying your life? Your work for instance. Your words touch so many people. Often those who seem to have no voice of their own. It's not selfish to take pleasure in that."

He smiled. "And I'm still writing that novel that will fire up the world, don't forget?" He grinned and took another sip of his martini. "How about you, Katie? You're in a bad place right now, but separate from that do you feel fulfilled?" Steve set down his glass at once. "Sorry," he said. "What a dumb question. Sort of like asking Mrs. Lincoln, 'But aside from that, did you enjoy the play?'"

"Similar, I'd say." Katie picked up her glass and Steve looked at her a few seconds as though carefully considering what he wanted to say next.

"Something else is on my mind," he said, finally. "I know we're solid friends. I know you admire my work. We think alike and laugh at the same things. But I feel far more than that for you. So I wonder where that leaves me."

Katie took a long slow breath, trying to adjust to his unexpected, blunt, unlike Steve, question. The scene with Sidney snuggled up to him had left Katie feeling vulnerable and likely to say more than she intended. "You're an amazing man in my eyes, Steve. You've been my rock of strength ever since we met. Always there for me."

Steve gazed into his martini glass in silence waiting for her to continue.

"At the moment all I ask from life is to keep my sanity during the next six months." Feeling awkward and not knowing where to go next, Katie told him something she'd thought many times. "Oh, my God, how I wish we'd met before my life became so damn complicated, Steve."

"But let's say your life will become less complicated one day." He stopped and took another sip of his drink. "Please keep an open mind for a minute or so now…And be honest…Have you ever envisioned us as more than friends? I mean imagined it?" He reached over and touched her hand and smiled broadly. "Fantasized us involved in a hot torrid romantic relationship?"

"Wow. Yes." She picked up her martini and took a healthy sip. "Have I? Many times," she said. "But you had to know that. I thought it was an unspoken secret between us." She felt herself getting flushed and beautifully warm all over. She squeezed his hand and smiled. "And what I imagine is always better than anything I've experienced before."

He laughed and then she laughed and he said, "Me too. Fantastic."

She paused a second or two and studied his face. "But why would *you* want *me*, Steve?" she asked him. "I'm trouble. I have so many unanswered questions about these last few years. Confusion about my own actions and inactions. I have a legal mess ahead of me."

"'Cos I knew you were my kind of woman the first day you strolled into the *Gazette*. I'm nuts about you, Katie."

He got up, came around and slid into the booth next to her. He put his arm around her shoulder. "I know I'm pushing you too hard. And being selfish. Sorry." He picked up her hand and kissed it.

"You're not pushing me anywhere I wouldn't like to go. But I couldn't treat you fairly this minute. I can't give you what you deserve right now. And I would be self-centered to ask you to be patient until I can."

"Don't worry, Katie. Continue the journey you're on. I'll try to be waiting for you at your destination."

"If you're there I'll welcome you with open arms," she said and he pulled her closer to him so she could rest her head on his shoulder.

She looked up at him and grinned. "But what about Sidney?"

"Who's Sidney?" Steve said, and they both laughed again. She picked up her glass. "Let's drink a toast to us."

* * * * * * *

Katie decided she had to see Jeff's partially completed house, not sure why but knowing if she didn't she'd always have been curious. She flipped through an outdated magazine in her room at the Wayfarer Inn, an historic Federalist home, now a bed and breakfast in Stone Harbor, the village a few miles south of the construction site. With their final divorce only months away, she thought there was another reason as well that she'd come. She hoped that seeing Jeff resettled would allow her more peace of mind to get on with her own life.

The next morning she waited for Jeff in her car in front of the Inn. As planned, he drove up and waved to her to follow him. They drove north on the coastal highway for about ten minutes and arrived in Stone Harbor, a village encircled by rocky cliffs and a thumbprint shaped harbor. A white steeple church atop a hill began an incline onto Main Street where a Rexall Drugstore on one side had a Greyhound Bus sign plastered to the inside of its window and on the other side was an IGA store, a hardware store and a spirits and wine shop. From Main Street narrow roads winding down to boat wharfs hosted the usual clusters of gift shops and waterfront restaurants.

Leaving the village and heading a few miles further north, the gray blue Atlantic Ocean was on the right. On the left, dry wall stone fences formed long gray necklaces across grassy meadows. Dirt roads wormed their way through the flat land toward clapboard barns and white frame houses. Struck by the orderliness of it all, Katie was reminded of Minnesota. She assumed the same sturdy people would be living here, enjoying their warm summers while preparing for winter blizzards and frigid temperatures by stocking food in pantries and freezers and storing candles in drawers. Instead of giving her comfort, though, this similarity left her feeling rootless today.

When Jeff turned off the highway onto a private road and started to drive to the precipice of a steep hill she felt anxious suddenly. Wondering why she had taken the word of Jeff's therapist that this would be all right, she reached into her purse and touched the dispenser of pepper spray that her own Dr.

Henry had insisted she bring along. "If you're determined to go through with this foolhardy act," he had insisted.

Taking in a long slow breath, Katie parked next to Jeff's car at the edge of a cliff and caught her first sight of the view, a finger of blue reaching inward to the land further west, and, in the other direction, water widening and opening up to the ocean.

She got out of her car, and seeing Jeff walk toward her, recalled the last time she'd laid eyes on him in the *Gazette* parking three months earlier. Tiny lines at the corners of his eyes and mouth seemed to have smoothed out since then. He smiled at her now extending his hand, then letting it fall to his side. If he hadn't pulled back, she would have probably grabbed hold of it. This wasn't going to be easy – stopping herself from doing what had been so natural.

She tried hard to picture him as he'd been that afternoon at the captain's house before she left for Minnesota. But damn, all she saw was the sun streaking through trees, hitting his high cheekbones and highlighting the violet of his eyes. She was probably missing more warning clues as she had done before, but he simply looked lonely, not treacherous, standing there. "Breathtaking view," she said.

"Glad you like it." He paused. "It's good to see you again, Katie."

"You're looking better. More at ease," she told him.

"I feel calmer. I'm going to stick with my therapy, whatever else happens." He smiled, letting their eyes meet. "You've changed too."

"Yes, I have."

"More the Katie I first met," he said. "I guess your sabbatical from me has been good medicine."

"Feeling much better, thank you," she said. Not magical, she admitted to herself, but better. "I was in a horrid state when I flew to Minnesota."

"I did that to you. Never letting you stand your ground with me. Throwing fits as if you were an enemy."

Not wanting to get into any of that today and sensing now that it would be safe to go inside, she said, "Let's walk up the path toward the house."

At the top of the hill, she got her first glimpse of the partly finished home rising up at the edge of the cliff, its solarium windows glinting under the sun's rays, gray clapboard exterior sprouting up from the center of a gathering of evergreen trees. Jeff swept an arm to the side and pointed to the foundation of a separate structure. "That's for a guest house for visitors and college kids' home for the weekend."

Pulling open the heavy wooden entrance door to the main house, he led her upstairs into a cathedral roofed living room and dining area separated from the kitchen by a long wooden bar. Then he brought her out onto a deck that circled the front and one side of the house. The view, even more startling from this second level, extended yet further east past a group of small islands and then out to sea. Placing her hands on the deck railing, Katie breathed in the salt air, a sea breeze blowing her hair back from her face. She turned around. "It is wonderful, Jeff."

He smiled, surely from his sense of achievement. "You approve?"

"I approve. You should be proud of your creation."

Her trepidations concerning possible danger had evaporated entirely. They walked downstairs and through the master bedroom and dressing room and then back out to their cars. Katie took one last look back at the house where she could easily have imagined herself living, cooking in that kitchen, warming herself by the Swedish woodstove, sleeping in the roomy master bedroom. She turned away at once. Torturing herself this way was almost masochistic, for heaven's sake.

"Do you have to go back tonight?" Jeff asked.

"I must," she said. He did seem different, most striking was the way he was letting this visit progress on its own. In the past, he'd have come armed with reservations at a lovely waterfront restaurant. He smiled at her and she said, "But, I suppose I could stay long enough for lunch."

"Great. There are a lot of good restaurants. Anything you're in the mood for?"

A place with no ambience, no atmosphere at all, is what she was thinking. "Something simple," she said. "Fish and chips would be good." She brushed a hand over her shirt and jeans. "I'm not dressed for gourmet."

The water, smooth as glass that day, barely moved two small rowboats tied to the restaurant wharf. Katie glanced away from the window and back at Jeff. They'd already discussed each of the children. Although Jeff had hired Mrs. Lewis as a full time housekeeper after Katie left he was obviously feeling taxed by now having total responsibility for three teenagers. Still, he hadn't pressured Katie in the way she feared with declarations of how much they needed her. She had gotten past some of her own guilt regarding the kids by continuing their therapy sessions with Dr. Henry. Incredibly, a month earlier, Mathew had found the courage to tell Jeff about their secret therapy, and Jeff, to Katie's astonishment, had agreed to let them go on seeing Dr. Henry. He had even insisted that he pay for their treatment. After their hour of therapy each week, she and the kids continued to have dinner together at the Chilli Pepper.

Katie glanced out the window at the strangely still water. Having already caught up on the children's lives, Katie could think of nothing more to say. Every subject but the kids she feared would take her down a path she didn't want to travel.

Interrupting her thoughts, Jeff said, "Your mind seems to have drifted away. I don't blame you. To tell you the truth, I wouldn't mind making up conversation with you for hours, but there's only one thing I really want to say. And that's how sorry I am about everything."

"I can never forget the violence you directed at me," Katie said while hating to reconnect to their past at all. "Frightening things come back, flashing before me as though they were happening for the first time."

In the past, Jeff would have accused her of being dramatic. Now he said, "How could you forget? I understand."

"I see you're trying to do things differently," she said, then stopped to take a drink from her water glass. "But I must make one thing clear to you. I don't want you to think we can get together like this back in Barrington. I can't do that."

"I don't expect to see you in Barrington," he answered quickly. "I'm just grateful you came to see the house."

Outside the restaurant, Jeff shifted his weight from one foot to the other. "Thanks for coming," he said opening her car door. "Let me know if you'd like to see the house again when I start to furnish it and landscape."

She got into her car and glanced back at him as he called out to her: "Have a safe drive back."

She waved goodbye, but alone again, felt disoriented and vowed to make only good choices from here on. But could she trust her judgment to be better now? One day in her *New Times* office in San Francisco, Leslie, her new assistant, had asked her to describe Jeff and Katie had told her without hesitation: "Oh, he's dependable and protective, level headed, intelligent, funny, romantic, and, by the way, good looking." A year earlier, before meeting Jeff, had someone asked her to describe her ideal man, she would have answered "someone bright, issue oriented, curious, quick witted and sexy to my eyes and touch."

Even this minute, she wasn't sure why Jeff had replaced that earlier person. Had it been his maturity? His seemingly down to earth attitude toward life? Had he made her feel safe having been surrounded by civil protest of one kind or another during most of her time in San Francisco? Even though she'd participated in the rebellion herself, perhaps Jeff had been a welcome respite from so much upheaval? Or, was it mostly the way he used to walk slowly toward her, wrapping his arms around her, bringing her head to rest on his chest, smoothing her hair almost unconsciously with one hand, as they finished a conversation?

Damn! That was then. Who is he now? Shit! Nothing about him had frightened her in the least all morning. Nothing! Why the hell couldn't he have brought about this metamorphosis earlier when all she wanted was a decent husband and a good marriage?

Chapter Thirteen

Helping Jeff pick out furniture for the new house seemed a good way to support his intentions to get on with his life. But now, examining pieces in a Stone Harbor showroom, Katie was having second thoughts as Jeff pulled a checkbook from his pocket and offered it to her. "You can sign the check," he said. "I opened a joint account. They had your signature on file from the last time you asked me to open one."

"No thank you. You shouldn't have done that," Katie said, backing away from his outstretched hand.

"Sorry, I didn't mean to embarrass you. The checkbook was just my stupid attempt to do something I should have done long ago," Jeff said. "I see it was an inappropriate thing to do now." While putting the checkbook back into his pocket, he motioned to a salesman who hurried across the room with an open invoice pad. "I'll order whatever the lady has chosen," he told him.

Jeff turned back to Katie. "Do you still want to stop at the house for lunch?"

"Of course," she said.

Katie drove a mile or so down the coast following Jeff's car. The ocean, gray-blue on an October morning, seemed to accentuate vibrant reds, oranges, and yellow foliage along the route. In spite of the checkbook mishap, the lovely day and her mission to help Jeff had left her feeling more hopeful that they could remain friends of some kind in the future.

Jeff trailed after Katie from one area to another in the new house while assuring him that his purchases would be perfect. "Thanks to you," he said moving into the living room area. "I'll start a fire and then make some sandwiches."

Later, finishing her lunch on the slate floor near the woodstove, Katie shivered. "Brrr. Your fire seems to be going out."

Jeff stood up, picked up a poker, and pulling the latch on the Swedish stove to the side, opened the door. He glanced back at Katie. "Would you like to learn how to keep a woodstove fire alive?"

"Sure," she said.

"Come over here then. Let me show you. Shove the logs around and stir up some embers with the poker until you get them sparking underneath. When a flame flares up, you put another log on top, but don't smother the flame underneath. Here, I'll show you." He crouched down and held her arm while she poked at the simmering fire until a small blue flame escaped from below and darted up through the space between two charred logs. "Quick now, grab a new log off the pile and stick it in there."

"With my bare hand?"

"Yes, quick. Toss it toward the back. That's the way. Now get another one and do the same and close the door. Now refasten the latch. Good, okay, now slide the lever under the door to the left to open the vent and let it breathe a minute."

Still kneeling alongside her, he backed up to let her finish. "When it really gets going, close the vent halfway."

A fat red flame suddenly took hold billowing upward from the new log. Katie twisted around to half close the vent and threw her arms in the air. "Great! I did it," she shouted.

Jeff sat down next to her. "Good work," he said and then, hesitating for a moment, said, "I hope you know I meant for us to have a great marriage, Katie. I fell in love with you as you

155

were. I don't know why I tried to turn you into somebody else."

She started to move away, but he reached over and set his hand on her shoulder. "Dr. Sherman believes I feared your strength and that I was scared your suggestions would upset my own dogged plans. I'm ashamed of that now." He dropped his hand from her shoulder and held a palm to his forehead. "I suppose I've lost you for good."

"You're trying to change. That's good for you, no matter where you go from here," she said. In her mind, she'd called him every nasty name she knew when first leaving him. Called herself a few too for acting the fool. "Keep on with what you're doing. For yourself, Jeff."

Telling herself to leave it there, she stood up and brushed off the crumbs from her jeans. Seeing him this way, more a kitten than king of the jungle, she was tempted to lean over, place a hand on his cheek and assure him he was going to be okay. But she couldn't do anything to make him *feel* better; it was up to him to *get* better. This reasoning gave her a breezy sense of freedom suddenly and she swung her purse over her shoulder and smiled down at him. "I have to leave now. Hope the furniture works out fine."

A few nights later, still half asleep, Katie reached for a ringing phone in the bedroom. "Hi, Katie?" An excitement in Jeff's voice alerted her she'd better wake up fast. She glanced at the clock on a nightstand and saw that it was after midnight. "I just flew in from New York," he said. "Guess what? I found some capital for you to start your magazine. Enough to buy a computer and office equipment with enough left for printing and doing a first mailing." He exhaled. "Whew! If you still want to do it, that is."

Bolting up, she sat on the edge of the bed. "How did you ever...?"

He paused a moment. "I imagine you're not thinking too far ahead these days. But please let me tell you my other idea." She got out of bed and pressed her back to the bedroom wall and waited for his next pronouncement. "I'm willing to buy a condo in Boston for you to use as an office. If you're interested. Up to you. All your decision naturally."

Sliding back onto the bed, Katie said, "I'm stunned. I haven't absorbed any of this yet." Then she laughed. "For once, one of your bulletins is making me smile."

"I love to hear you sounding happy again. No hurry. Let me know."

She hung up the phone, went out to Natalie's kitchen, made herself tea and spent much of the night mulling over Jeff's offer while questioning his possible motives for making it. She realized that asking Jeff too many questions might lose her a one-time opportunity, but then, an offer with strings would be no offer at all.

Isn't this what she had intended to do with the money she received from the sale of her San Francisco flat all along? That is before Jeff talked her into contributing half the down payment on the captain's house? And using much of what was left to pay daily household expenses? So yes, she decided she could gladly accept his gesture as a return of money that she'd used on his behalf. Only she would have to clarify that any money she received from him now was a return of her own funds. She had no wish to feel beholden to him.

No denying that a chance to try her luck with the publication could be the fresh start she needed. *But calm down,* she told herself. Things have to be clarified before getting too excited.

At daylight, she called Jeff back and got straight to the point. "I need to be frank, Jeff. I'm happy you're making me this offer, but you must first know this: I will consider this money to be repayment to me for expenses I incurred on behalf of you and your kids and for my half of the down payment on the captain's house. And also for having given up a good paying job in San Francisco to be with you.

"In addition, I want to be clear on this: I alone am responsible for this venture. I wouldn't be agreeing to any conditions beyond a contract stating the amount you've repaid me. I hope you aren't offended by my frankness. Better to have things said and in writing than a misunderstanding later." She took a breath. "So what do you think?"

"I know you've suffered financially on my account, Katie. Call this payback of a loan if you're comfortable with that. I should have helped you in the beginning before letting you spend so much of your own money. Of course, this is your undertaking."

"I have no more plans for us to reconcile than I had before today."

"I understand."

"Then I agree. I'd like to do it."

* * * * * * *

That same morning Katie sidled up to Steve's desk and slipped into a nearby chair. She was anxious to tell him her news but nervous that he would be unhappy about Jeff's involvement in her life, if only on a financial level.

"Steve I have something big to tell you," she said. "But please promise you will listen to all the facts before offering an opinion."

"Sure. Whatever it is, I'm all ears."

He listened but by the time she finished his smile had faded. "What did you think I'd say? I care about you, Katie. I want your dreams to come true. But I worry any time you mention seeing Jeff for any reason. I don't trust the guy; I wish you'd never ever speak to him again. Listen to me, if you do this, he'll be all over your daily business. I wish you'd continue to heal yourself as you've been doing so well. Your divorce is only months off. Jeff will have to settle with you financially then anyway. I realize I have no right to tell you what to do. But, sorry, I have bad vibes about this out of the blue offer of his. You asked me what I thought."

"Steve, my morale needs a booster shot. My marriage has been a failure. I need a new challenge – something I might succeed at again. Once Jeff pays me the money and I purchase a condo in Boston, my dealings with him can be over. Finished."

"Get that point in writing," he said. Then frowning, he added, "Maybe you do need to prove something to yourself, but you've never had to convince me of your ability and talent."

"Please try to understand, Steve."

"I will always support you, Katie. Even when I think you're taking the wrong fork in the road. If you're hell bent on doing this, I can't stop you. But for God's sake, be careful. Wear a bullet proof vest when he gets within fifty yards of you."

* * * * * * *

A few weeks later, on a Saturday afternoon, Katie met Jeff in Boston to sign papers on a condo in a refurbished building on Atlantic Avenue. Afterward, they walked a block over to Hanover Street past the Old North Church with its steeple pointing upward to a cloudless sky. At the end of a cobblestone alley, they wandered into the Liberty Pub where Paul Revere and his comrades had plotted acts of rebellion two hundred years earlier.

Jeff smiled at her across a rough-hewn table. "So, you really like the condo?"

"Airy and light, the right size. Good location, convenient to downtown." She could already imagine herself working in this space with its immense windows offering a panoramic view of Boston Harbor from the living room and its rear windows looking down on this historic North End neighborhood.

"I take it that's a yes?"

"I feel like a kid who's won the biggest stuffed animal at the fair." Katie was proud to be trusting her instincts enough to make confident decisions again.

"You'll need a computer and file cabinets," he said, then brought an open hand to his mouth. "Habit. *You* know what you need." He swung his head around and hailed a waiter. "How about a corned beef sandwich to celebrate?"

"Good idea. But I'm almost too excited to eat."

* * * * * * *

"Disgustingly cheerful," Natalie commented on Monday morning as Katie described the Boston condo. "Promise me you won't break into 'the hills are alive with music'." She picked up a stack of mail from her in-box. "Nice that you liked the condo, but I hate that you're leaving us and moving to Boston."

"It's not that far. Have Nathan come up from New York. You can both stay with me over a weekend."

"Okay." Natalie glanced up from her papers. "Do you *actually* think you and Jeff have become friends?"

"Yes. I'm amazed but it's true. And it's happened within a few months' time."

Steve ambled into Natalie's office. "What about the condo?"

"I'm taking it," Katie answered.

"I see," he said, then turned around to leave. Over his shoulder, he said, "Let's talk later, Katie."

Natalie frowned. "I guess we're being too hard on you, but we're both worried as hell."

"Why couldn't I have married someone like Steve in the first place? Then nobody would have to worry about me. Not even me."

"I'll bet Steve is thinking the same thing this very minute."

"I'll talk to him again and assure him I'll be fine," Katie said.

* * * * * * *

A month later, seated in the Catch Tavern with Natalie and Steve, Katie admitted, "I'm getting very nervous now that I'm not all talk."

Steve pushed his empty chowder bowl aside. "I hope Jeff doesn't have a key to your place. If he does, change the locks. Stay safe." He'd repeated this warning every day since she'd made her decision.

Katie reached across the table to touch Steve's hand. "Jeff has no expectations of me personally. None whatsoever!"

"Remember that," Natalie said.

"Remember, I plan to help you with the editing," Steve said.

His effort to be more upbeat made her leaving more difficult. "I hope you won't be sorry you offered."

"Hey, smile, Katie," he said lifting his beer bottle in a toast. "I don't want to dampen your enthusiasm. You're going to enjoy putting this publication together. *Ms, Lear* and now...by the way, what are you going to call it?"

"Blind Faith, Chasing Moonbeams?"

Steve smiled. "What about Tenacity? Hey, call me as soon as you get to Boston tonight."

"Steve, I won't even have a phone hooked up until tomorrow. Okay, I'll call you from a pay phone. I'm not the beaten down person I was when I first knocked on your door all those months ago, Natalie. I'll be okay." She traced her index finger around the nozzle of her bottle. "I'm going to miss seeing both of you every day." She took a sip of beer. "But we'll drive back and forth."

Outside, standing next to Katie's car, Steve reached both arms around her and kissed her on the on the cheek. "I want you to be successful. Only take care."

"I will," she promised before turning to give Natalie a hug.

Steve put his arms around Katie again and held her close and then opened her car door. She blew them a kiss out the window and drove out of the parking lot in her car packed with clothes and duffle bags.

Heading north on I-95 toward the Northeast Expressway, her decision seemed entirely real for the first time. An hour and a half later, she exited at Atlantic Avenue and drove toward the renovated wharf building that would house her office and new little home. Some furniture from the captain's house, a bed and table, four chairs and a desk would be delivered in the morning. That's all she wanted from the dark caverns of that dreadful place. This could be a good life, she concluded again, hanging out and working in Boston, the San Francisco of the east, and seeing her friends in Barrington often.

* * * * * * *

Two days before Christmas, snuggled into a lounge chair in her condo living room, Katie wrapped her hands around a coffee mug to warm them. No question, she felt satisfied with her accomplishments so far in Boston. She'd compiled a list of possible subscribers and contacted several potential advertisers and by next spring, would have completed the research on some important articles. At this rate, with Steve's help editing freelance pieces, the first edition of *Moving On* could be ready for printing by next fall.

She and Jeff had spoken by phone several times, mostly to compare their news of the children. But a week ago he had called to invite her to spend a couple of days in the new home over Christmas. He'd put Mathew and Tommy and Martha on a plane to California to spend the holidays with their mother and Robert had decided to stay in New York. "This means I'll be alone in Stone Harbor. Any chance we could keep each other company if you haven't made other holiday plans?" he had asked, saying that she could use the master bedroom and that he would stay in the guest house.

Steve had invited her to join him at his family's home in Connecticut for the holidays but she told him she would rather meet his parents when her personal life wasn't so disrupted. Natalie and Nathan would of course be together in New York. So Jeff's offer looked rather inviting to her now on the day before Christmas Eve. She'd been awake much of the night wondering whether or not to take Jeff up on his offer. Steve and Natalie would think it was a bad idea but they didn't get the sort of friendship she now had with Jeff.

Finally, about 4:00 a.m. she had decided she would go. Now, however, downing her second cup of coffee, she started to have doubts. So much in her life had improved since she'd been separated from Jeff. She remembered how only a year ago, Jeff was bemoaning the fact that one day his children would be leaving home. Katie smiled now: that, of course, was while she was still there to oversee them on a daily basis. This past September Martha was the only one to move with her father into the new home in Stone Harbor. In another year, even she would be departing early for prep school in Connecticut. Mathew had left for the University of Rhode Island in September and later in the fall, Jeff had managed to find a room and board high school in Providence for Tommy where Mathew could keep an eye on him during his last two years of high school.

Her thoughts swayed back to the captain's house now and immediately a chill rippled across her shoulders. She no longer fooled herself about the original purpose of that big draughty mansion. Jeff had chosen it for himself and his children, not her. The new house could have been a different story. Jeff and his architect had designed it; she had met Jeff twice more after purchasing the furniture to help him choose kitchen appliances, cabinets, and carpeting. Doing this, however, had made it harder to shake a persistent notion that had things not turned out so dastardly, this new home would have *really* belonged to Jeff and her. They might have made room for a nursery for the baby of their own that they never had – the baby she'd stopped thinking about while coping with a house full of Jeff's kids.

She shot a hand to her mouth suddenly and gasped. *Stop this, Katie. Don't let yourself get sucked into that messy nostalgic quicksand, for God's sake.*

Glancing around her modern condo living room she suddenly felt safe again. She threw back her head and sighed. *I'm doing all right now and glad of it. Walking with a surer gait. Jeff has never raised his voice to me or said a mean thing to me during all our months of separation...*

I am no longer afraid of him, she realized for the first time.

Setting her coffee mug aside, Katie got up, went to the bedroom and reached for her overnight bag on the closet shelf.

* * * * * * *

The next afternoon, Katie poked her head around the branches of a Christmas tree she and Jeff were struggling to drag up a slope to the house. "Are you sure we were allowed to cut this down?" She laughed. "Won't the tree police come up the hill in hot pursuit and haul us off to an environmental prison?"

"They'll never know," Jeff said, making a turn toward the house. "What are they going to do, count every tree in the county? Wait now. Let me open the front door wider. Look at this tree. It's probably the most perfect spruce tree in North America. You picked out a beauty, Katie. It's supposed to snow all night and half of tomorrow. Good thing we won't have to go outside. All we have to do is trim the tree."

Katie followed him and the tree he was now pulling up the stairs to the living room. "Lights and tinsel are all I could find," she said. "The rest of the ornaments must still be in the cellar of the captain's house."

"Which reminds me," Jeff said. "I have to get somebody to clean out that place so it can be sold. Well, never mind about that now. We can improvise our decorations." He hauled the tree into the living room and set it to the side of the solarium windows. "Can you make a star out of something for the top? I'll do the lights."

He held the tree by the trunk and turned it until she told him where to stop and then lifted the tree into the stand. "Here, take hold of this," he said. She grabbed the trunk tight with both hands and he bent over to tighten the screws. He looked up at her from his kneeling position and smiled. "You can let go now. It's securely planted."

"Let's have a cognac in the living room," Katie suggested after a mutually prepared dinner of sautéed shrimp and rice and asparagus that evening. They were alone in this home of angles and peaks and windows. It was going to snow for the next two days. Aware that the last cobwebs of her apprehension had disappeared hours ago had left her feeling somewhat disarmed. Jeff had apologized during lunch and asked her forgiveness that afternoon over coffee and then at dinner repeated his commitment to continue with his therapy as long as necessary.

She set a tray on the floor, gathered up pillows and nestled them on the thick carpet near the woodstove. Snow was still falling steadily, thousands of flakes in the moonlight dancing in slow motion outside the magnificent solarium windows. "What a show you've arranged, Jeff."

"My Christmas Eve Special. Glad you like it," he said, and then sat down on a pillow near her.

Remembering the way she used to fit into the corner of his shoulder, she envisioned resting her head there now. Certainly such a thought had not been part of her earlier plans. But this wasn't the first time, as Jeff seemed to be getting better, that she'd wondered if she could ever have *those* feelings toward him again. Then, ashamed, she had admonished herself – *Don't feel this, don't miss that, remember what he did to you.*

Now, as they watched the snow forming a thick curtain at the window, he reached his arm around her shoulder in the most comforting way. She thought of inching away from him, but didn't. "Do you think you could ever give me another chance, Katie?" he asked, his voice thinner than air. He swirled the cognac in his snifter glass and took a sip. Together, they kept gazing out at the flakes, larger now, sticking to the glass and shaping crescents at the window corners. He picked up her hand and held it to his chest. "I have a hell of a nerve. One hell of a nerve asking that."

"When I came back from Minnesota, I was sure there was no possibility you would ever change." She turned toward him. "I certainly didn't think we could ever be friends. To be truthful, Jeff, I might never be able to trust you all the way again. If you were to so much as drop a spoon in anger, I'd walk out on you. You wouldn't want someone that unsure of you. And besides, I'm used to living on my own again with absolute peace of mind. I like how that feels." She wanted him to know she was most satisfied with her present life at the moment.

"I would never frighten you like that again. But why should you believe me?"

"If I had a crystal ball that could promise me you would stay the way you are right now, I might...possibly...just possibly... feel differently." She placed her hand on his cheek. "But, I couldn't know that, could I?"

"Maybe in time you could believe in me again." He turned and lifted her face up with a finger under her chin. She didn't back away from him. Her thoughts seemed to have taken an unexpected detour asking improbable questions, *what if, just for tonight, we could be the way we once were – make love like that – one more time – perhaps to sooth old grievances?*

"I've missed you," he said. "Hell, I don't deserve to tell you that." He touched her cheek. "But still, I would like nothing more than to hold you in my arms again."

"Just for tonight?" she said in a whisper.

"If you like," he said, then turning to her, he placed his lips on hers and kissed her slowly, tenderly, much as they had the first time in California.

As the amber liquid in their glasses glowed pleasantly in the firelight, Katie let herself drift back to those confident trouble free days in the beginning. And sinking into the familiarity of his arms, she pretended. *Just for tonight.*

Chapter Fourteen

Katie crawled sleepily out of bed in a warm haze for a few seconds. And then the memory of what had happened the night before swept over her. She sat back down on the bed. Would she and Jeff interpret the event in the same way? He had said "one more time"; she had said, "Just for tonight". Meaningless, dispassionate words unbefitting the occasion, an excuse for immediate pleasure, she admitted now. She held her head in her hands. What the devil was she thinking? Not thinking, she meant. She threw her head back. Don't panic, for God's sake, she ordered herself. Go upstairs, have coffee, make breakfast, act confident.

"Good morning," Jeff said. He pulled out a stool. "Sit down. Breakfast's all ready."

"Oh, you should have waited. I would have helped. But it does look good."

"Eggs scrambled the way you like them."

"Jeff, about last night... Can we consider it one of those things that just happened? Maybe in the spirit of Christmas?"

He looked over at her and smiled. "If you like. Neither of us planned it. Anymore than we ordered up such a beautiful evening, the snowfall, the quiet privacy. We acted spontaneously, Katie. That's all. Don't regret this, please. You haven't lost a thing. You're the same free-spirited woman you were before yesterday. Let's just relax and enjoy the rest of today. What do you say?"

"I say I'm hungry."

"Let's eat then." He offered her a helping of scrambled eggs and cinnamon toast.

She took the plate from his hand. "Can we take a nice long drive this afternoon?" she asked. "It would be fun to view the snowy wonderland left behind by the Christmas Eve storm."

"Sure. And I know just the place to stop for a hot buttered rum on the way back before you have to leave for Boston."

* * * * * * *

Once back in Boston, Katie expected to find herself cloaked in self recriminations, perhaps mourning the possibility that she had lost moral ground with Jeff. When this didn't occur, she allowed for the likelihood that they had acted on an impulse and that was that. That night Jeff called to tell her she was welcome to visit whenever she needed a day away from the city. Feeling perfectly at ease with his ongoing invitation, Katie looked forward to returning the next time the children visited. If only we'd been able to create this sort of relaxed atmosphere in our marriage, Katie thought, but saw immediately how impossible that would have been considering she'd been married to a totally different person then.

With no pressure from Jeff to alter their present relationship, Katie took advantage of some casual visits to the house that spring. Eventually though, Katie realized that this arrangement could not last forever. As Jeff continued his therapy becoming more each day the man she had wanted so desperately, Katie questioned her own reluctance to move wholeheartedly toward a permanent reconciliation. Hadn't Jeff earned that much? Isn't this what she'd begged him to do during the worst times? Was she trashing his bravest effort to give her what she'd dreamed of earlier?

But how was she to explain any of this to Steve and Natalie? Embarrassed and feeling too awkward to speak to either of them she stopped returning their phone calls for a few weeks. One morning, hungry to catch up with her friends, she forced herself to dial Natalie's number.

"It's about time we heard from you," Natalie stated, her anger undisguised. "Where the hell have you been?"

Katie's honest revelations about her new relationship with Jeff created a long silence at the other end. Finally, Natalie muttered, "I'm sorry to hear that. Steve will be shattered. If I know Steve, and I do, he will suspect that Jeff is pressuring you to cancel the divorce."

"I'm torn up about Steve," Katie said. "I expect I may not hear back from him for a long time." She paused. "I hope not forever. I never imagined Jeff would evolve into the considerate person he's become. I know I stayed too long in a bad situation. I hated to fail at a marriage. But what if I'm divorcing a man who no longer exists?" Katie asked. "I'm feeling damn well guilty and thinking Jeff must deserve some credit for all his hard work and struggle to change. I must owe him for this, don't I?"

"Katie, I think some part of you wants to resuscitate feelings you once had for Jeff. And the divorce still represents a failure to you. And then, I suppose Jeff's seeming recovery means you might not have to acknowledge that failure. But it wasn't *your* failure, girl. I wish to hell you'd just accept that and give up on what didn't happen when you wanted it to."

"Okay. I agree, but poor guy, I feel obligated. I could try to love him again in his new mellow, compassionate state."

"I can't imagine Jeff like that. Keep in touch no matter how uncomfortable it feels, Katie. I'll answer your calls. I can't say the same for Steve. Let's just leave it at that for now."

That summer vanished pleasantly with Katie driving south to Stone Harbor on several Saturdays for an afternoon of sailing. By September, though, her planned projects, an interview with a Catholic missionary nun returned from El Salvador, a backgrounder piece on the Equal Rights Amendment and setting up her printing and mailing schedules had fallen behind. Unlike the old Jeff, the new Jeff merely shrugged his shoulders when she told him she would have to spend nearly all of her time in Boston that fall. "I understand," he said but the next Friday he drove up to Boston instead of remaining in Stone Harbor. On Saturday morning he paced outside Katie's office while she conducted phone interviews with a freelance writer, advertisers, and the printer. She planned to eat a quick snack at her desk but Jeff called her to the table at noon for a hearty soup and sandwich lunch. That afternoon he opened her office door every twenty minutes or so to ask, "Can I help you with anything?"

Finally, with her concentration shot, Katie gave up and walked a few blocks with him to an Italian coffee shop in the North End. Afterward, they took the Green Line subway to Copley Square and strolled over to the Charles River.

When they returned to her condo two hours later, Jeff fell into a chair and picked up the *Boston Globe*. "Guess I should stay in Stone Harbor next weekend," he said, glancing up at her. "I suppose I'm driving you crazy here, don't you agree? I could drive up to Boston on Sunday night, though, if that's okay with you. And drive back to Barrington Monday morning in time for work."

"If you want to come, I guess Sunday night would be okay." she said, astounded that he was going to follow her to her Boston workplace. She swept her hand over a pile of papers on her desk and said, "I'm doing everything myself except for the typing and proofing the temp agency does. Talk about naïve, thinking I could accomplish all this by myself.

When the writing is finished, I still have to design the cover page and get out the mailing." She wiped her hand across her forehead. "If I'm successful enough to do a second issue, I'll definitely hire an assistant."

Jeff walked over to her and set his hand on her shoulder. "I'll have to get used to your being off in your own little world, won't I?" he said.

His phrase "off in her own little world" kept worming its way into Katie's consciousness on Monday, rankling her as it produced an infuriating image of a young girl skipping through sunny meadows tossing daisy petals to the wind. She tried to shrug it off thinking maybe she was being overly sensitive and remembering the old Jeff. In any case she would have to stop herself from feeling torn between Jeff and her work again.

Jeff arrived the following Sunday evening and stated immediately that he'd been lonely in Stone Harbor that weekend. Then he held out his arms to Katie and held her in a bear hug. "It's strange having no kids in the house for the first time and I missed not having you there Saturday. I guess I'm just feeling at loose ends."

"You mean you're restless? You're keeping your appointments with Dr. Sherman, aren't you?"

"I've cut back to every other week."

Katie drew in a breath. "Oh, you promised him you'd go every week."

He moved around her and, placing his hands at the back of her neck, started to massage between her shoulder blades. "Your muscles are tight. You should get up from that computer more often." He sighed. "This is becoming a full-time job for me."

"What is?"

"Taking care of you. Now don't get stressed out over this project."

"I'm not stressed. Just busy. But I'm doing work I love." She bent forward. "That does feel wonderful. I think I'll be wrapping up this first edition in a matter of weeks now."

* * * * * * *

A week later, Katie gazed out at reflections of an autumn sun on Boston Harbor while hugging a phone to her ear. "Slow down," she said. "What did you say?"

"Katie, pay attention," Maxine ordered her from California. "I eloped this weekend."

"You did not. I don't believe you!"

"Shocked, aren't you? Me too. You know, Tony and I have been living together for months. So what the hell, we decided to get legalized. Spur of the moment, time to get the license and that was it.

"You have to come out and meet him. He's a lovable, recycled sixties guy wondering what happened to the revolution. Well, I wasn't going to fall for a stockbroker, was I? He had a minister lined up to marry us, but I grabbed him by the hand and dragged him down to the marriage bureau at Berkeley City Hall before either of us could change our minds. Then we drove up to Tahoe and stayed in somebody or other's cabin."

"Oh, I wish I'd been there."

"When are you coming out? I've waited way too long already."

"I'll come out for Christmas." Katie loved the way she was relaxed enough to say this for the first time. "Jeff might tag along, though. He can visit his kids who will be out there with their mother for the holidays."

"Do you believe he's really been rehabilitated? How can you be sure? Seems impossible after what he did."

"He's different all right. More like that person I fell in love with in California."

"He must have the best damn shrink in the country. He's lucky you're even speaking to him. I hope your divorce is still in the works."

"Yes, but I'm conflicted. Jeff and I are getting along and he's made such an effort to change. It just seems unfair to bail out on him now."

"That makes me nervous, Katie. You have to make your own decisions but think long and hard before you do something stupid."

"Okay, but can I change the subject for a second? As you know, I'm getting close to launching my first, albeit mini size, edition of a publication." Katie laughed. "A few years late, but never mind. I'll be crazy until December. By the way, can I send you some stuff to read? I'd appreciate your opinion. God, why am I bothering you with this now? On your honeymoon? Geez, it hasn't sunk in yet. I'm dumbstruck. But thrilled for you. Don't suppose you're changing your name?"

"Nah. I'm crazy about him, but not that crazy. But back to you. Whatever you do, Katie, don't you dare forget to cover your ass this time."

"The truth is, I'm enjoying being in charge of my life again. And for once I don't seem to need ass covering."

"Hey, our asses always need covering. That's a given. Don't forget it. Can't wait to see you. How about I get Peter, Paul and Mary to serenade you at the airport for old times' sake?"

Katie laughed. "I love you, Maxine. Congratulations. To Tony, too."

She put down the phone and whistled. "Whew, Maxine married." How she longed to visit San Francisco and see Maxine and old co-workers from *New Times*, whoever was still there, and some of the old peaceniks and McGovernites, too. Maxine would know where to find them all.

* * * * * *

Finally, on a December afternoon six weeks later, Katie sprinted down Boylston Street to her parked car. With the interviews, the writing, the courting of advertisers, the fighting with printers, all finished, she had just delivered the last boxes of her periodical to the Post Office. She could let herself dream now that with a whole lot of luck her publication would one day become an actual slick magazine. She got in her car, slammed the door, and shouted, "Damn, I did it!" and headed south to Stone Harbor. Shoot, if she were Jeff she would be taking deep drags on a giant cigar about now.

"Congratulations!" he called out as he rushed from the house to meet her car in the driveway. "I made reservations at the Atlantic House to celebrate with you tonight."

Nothing that evening could have brought Katie down to earth, not even a sturdily built blonde unhappy looking woman at a nearby table who couldn't seem to take her eyes off them. Katie knew she herself must appear deliriously ecstatic to this woman or to anyone who happened to observe her at that moment. In fact, she felt sorry for anybody who was sad this evening when she was feeling so absolutely indomitable.

In bed the next morning, Katie listened to the comforting hum of Jeff's deep morning breathing. He was going to have her undivided attention in California for the next two weeks. Too excited to sleep late, she slipped carefully out of bed. In another week, she would be seeing her old San Francisco friends. And Jeff had made reservations to revisit the inn near Mendocino, the one with the stone Buddha at its entrance and tremendous fireplace and smoky aroma inside, where their intimate relationship had begun. If anything could put her in a sentimental mood, Katie supposed it would be reliving the memory of that first night together. Surely something had to renew her faith in marriage and her belief in a man who has taken heroic measures to try to regain her love.

Letting a fresh cup of coffee wake her, she wondered how much Maxine will have changed. Of course she wouldn't look like the picture of her that Katie had carried around in her head since leaving California almost three years ago -- the image that persisted in spite of new photographs that had arrived every so often in the mail. Whenever Katie heard Maxine's voice on the telephone, she continued to see her in a peasant skirt and shawl, honey blonde hair parted down the center and flowing half way down her back.

"I talked to Maxine yesterday," Katie told Jeff who had just come upstairs and pulled out a stool next to her at the bar. She reached for the carafe and poured coffee into his mug. "You wouldn't believe the plans she and Tony are making for us. A welcoming party, lunch, dinners. They will be waiting at the gate when we arrive. They're still threatening to have Peter, Paul and Mary there as well to greet us." She grinned at Jeff. "You'd love that, wouldn't you?"

"Say they're joking," he said. "By the way, I have to attend a dinner tomorrow night in honor of Caroline Martin. She's the psychiatric social worker who conducted the fund drive for the new Stone Harbor counseling center." He patted Katie's hand. "You don't have to go, but I'd better show up. I met her at the village council meeting I attended a few weeks back. She wants me to serve on the board of the new center. Never hurts to ingratiate one self to the locals." He smiled at Katie, eyebrows raised, the way he always did when he thought he'd done something clever.

"My, you've been busy, haven't you?" Katie said. "I'll go to the dinner. I'd like to meet her."

"She's quite a prestigious person around these parts."

Katie got up from her stool at the bar and kissed Jeff on the cheek. "You want me to curtsy for her? I will, if you want me to."

"Go easy, woman. Our reputation is at stake here."

* * * * * * *

The guest of honor, gathered up and surrounded by admirers at the door, was hidden from Katie's view at first. When the group parted, Katie was surprised to recognize her as the same blonde woman who'd sat near them in the restaurant two nights earlier and stared at them all evening. Knowing who she was made her earlier behavior seem even more strange.

"You aren't going to believe this," Katie said, nudging Jeff. "Dr. Martin is the woman I felt sorry for in the restaurant the other night."

"No, it couldn't have been her," he said.

"Yes, it was her. You had your back to her." She took Jeff's hand. "Since you've met her, introduce me."

"Later. It's time to find our table now."

"Nobody's seated yet," Katie said, taking Jeff's hand and guiding him across the room.

"Caroline?" Jeff tapped the woman's shoulder.

Caroline spun around and Katie noted that she had brightened up considerably since dining by herself, full lips now opening into a broad smile, eyes downright sparkly. Grasping Jeff's arm, Caroline started to walk away with him. "Come Jeff, there are people I want you to meet." Jeff looked helplessly over his shoulder. Katie first watched his capture in amusement, then quickly stepped forward and wove her fingers into his free hand.

"Ah, Caroline," Jeff said. "I'd like you to meet my wife." He stepped aside. "Katie, Caroline Martin."

"Oh, I didn't notice you..." Caroline said, giving Katie a quick glance and sliding backward a foot or so. "Excuse me. I have so many other guests to greet."

Katie shrugged her shoulders. With a quick half turn, Jeff led her away from Caroline and her group and over to their designated table. Jeff was ordinarily in good form at affairs like this, almost nothing preventing him from shaking hands and pronouncing his name clearly for people. She didn't relish seeing him look uncomfortable, but still there was something humorous about the way this woman had sent him running.

Glancing around at the obviously well-heeled population of this coastal community, Katie yearned for a friendly spot at the end of a wharf where she could hang out in jeans and sweater with some friends and talk to a few lobster fishermen or some dockworkers. She set her hand on Jeff's shoulder and gave him a sympathetic look. "Don't feel badly. I think it's me she doesn't care for, not you. I probably remind her of a patient she couldn't cure."

Jeff smiled half-heartedly and sat down. "She's something of a princess around here," he said fidgeting with his place setting. "Can do no wrong. Her daddy owns a couple of furniture factories and a resort up in Bar Harbor, Maine. But we'll need to have her on our side."

For what, Katie wondered? Sneaking a sideways peak at Jeff, she gathered that this was no joking matter with him. In fact, he might be cold sober about making a place for himself in this new community. She glanced at him again; he was concentrating harder on his place setting, lining up the silver for military inspection it would appear. Katie introduced Jeff and herself to other guests joining their table and tried to start conversations that seemed to go nowhere. Was it her imagination, or had their table happened to draw a particularly tight-ass group?

The moment the dinner and the award presentation to Caroline were over, Jeff hustled Katie out of the restaurant. Once in the car, he reached for her hand. "Sorry," he said. "I don't know why Caroline was so discourteous."

Katie smiled; she wished Jeff could see the entertainment value in this curious affair. "As though I care?" she said. "She seems to be an odd person. In fact, this was a weird evening all around, if you ask me."

Chapter Fifteen

Katie carried Christmas gifts for Maxine and Tony and the kids who were already in San Francisco into the house and dropped the packages on the master bed. "There. Now all we have to do is pack our suitcases in a couple of days."

She flopped onto the bed as Jeff poked his head out of the dressing room. "What's this?" she asked, picking up a paperback book from his night table. *The Love Addiction: Breaking Co-Dependency.* "Doesn't sound like your kind of reading."

He came over to the bed, lifted the book from her hand and tossed it back onto the night table. "I'll explain it to you when you're older."

"Seriously, 'love addiction', Jeff?"

"It's about people who do too much giving in a love relationship."

"Such as?" she asked, a little startled since Dr. Henry had always described her that way.

"Well. I'm aware of my tendencies," he said.

His tendencies? Katie willed herself not to smile. Surely, Dr. Sherman hadn't accused Jeff of "giving too much" even in his improved state, had he?

"Guess I'll have to read the book, won't I?" she said. "By the way, I'll have to use your car to pick up our mail at the post office, Jeff. My old Chevy is acting up again."

* * * * * * *

Katie pushed the latch under the driver's seat and adjusted mirrors to accommodate herself and started the engine. On her way to the post office she thought about the book she'd found on Jeff's nightstand. Giving too much? Katie laughed out loud this time. A good thing she had never expected Jeff to be her caretaker. Once she'd had to go to the doctor with an extreme case of stomach flu and Jeff had glanced up from his crossword puzzle just long enough to advise her: "Drive carefully if you're feeling dizzy." No, he wouldn't have ever qualified as a co-dependent sort of person. Well, so what? Let him see himself any way he chooses, she thought. What's the difference?

Returned from the post office, she reached across to the passenger seat to pick up the mail but her finger scraped across an object that had lodged between the seat and the console. She dug out what turned out to be a lipstick, unscrewed the top and examined it.

Surely there must be an explanation for a bright red lipstick being caught in the upholstery of Jeff's car, Katie thought. But unable to think of one offhand, she ran into the guesthouse and dropped her find on top of a stack of papers on Jeff's desk. He gazed down at it without speaking and she wanted to shout, "Say something. Don't just sit there." As she waited a sense of dread started to penetrate her consciousness, making her clutch the edge of the desktop and hang on to it. Vital organs that made her blood flow and her lungs take in oxygen seemed to be closing down on her. *Please give me an explanation other than the one that is now scorching the edges of my world. Say anything. Say you kidnapped a wealthy Yankee heiress for ransom, say you robbed a bank and took a woman hostage. Tell me anything but what I'm thinking, please.*

"For heaven's sake, Katie," he said at last. "I gave this woman a ride home from the gym last weekend. It must have fallen from her pocket or purse."

"Who?" Katie asked, her voice sounding accusatory and not what she intended because she wanted to believe him.

He bowed his head, clamping a hand to his forehead. "Really, Katie. What difference does that make?"

"I'm curious, that's all."

He peered up at her through spread fingers and shook his head. She waited again, his silence more shrill than a scream.

"Are you having an affair?" she asked thinking of no subtle way to ask such a question.

No words could equal the sharp pain stabbing her in her gut now anyway. She closed her eyes and turned away from him and covered her face. He hadn't said, but she knew. She felt herself shutting down, possibly growing a second skin to protect herself from his eventual response. *This can't be happening* is all her mind could accept. *No, not this, after my trying so to trust again.*

He got up and came around the desk. She felt his hand on her shoulder, shrugged it off and slumped into a nearby chair. He kneeled on the carpet in front of her and let his head drop into her lap. Neither spoke for several seconds until Jeff whispered, "Come on, Katie. How could you ask such a thing?"

She gazed down at his drooping head and they went silent again.

Neither of them moved until Jeff spoke again, his voice dry and gritty now. "I was feeling jumpy. You were working so much. That project was consuming you."

"My God, I saw you when I could. You encouraged me to do the periodical, didn't you?"

"I didn't expect your work to shut me out again."

"When you offered to return my money you said you didn't expect anything of me, remember? No strings attached? I worked hard for a few months. I was on a deadline."

"But our relationship has changed since then? What's worse, I couldn't get rid of stress anymore the way I used to."

She held her hand to her chest and breathed hard. How had this turned around to criticism of her? Why was she on the carpet? No, she wasn't going to slip into that trap again. "You couldn't explode, so you had an affair? Is that what you're telling me?"

"No...I don't know. Maybe." He kept his head bowed. "You know I love you. I was feeling desperate."

She started to tune him out. "Who is she?" she asked to force herself back to this fresh disaster. Having a name might make this real. At the moment his words were drifting midair like strips of chiffon needing a place to light in order to take shape. He didn't answer. She pushed his head from her lap, got up, and feeling dizzy, wove her way unsteadily across the room and out of the guest house. He got up, ran to her, and cupping his arm under her elbow, helped her across the path to the main house and into the master bedroom. She lowered herself to the bed and he lay down beside her. A part of her wanted to turn to him and reclaim him for now. Another voice, stronger, forced her to move away from him and stare up at the ceiling.

She got up shortly and went upstairs and he followed her. He went to the kitchen sink and ran a glass of water. She glared at his back from where she stood on the other side of the bar. "Who is she, Jeff?"

He drank some water, turned around and then frowned at her. "Why do you care?" he said.

"I'm asking so it must be important to me. It's not a difficult question." The biting ache inside her body had turned her voice shrill. Her skin felt paper thin as if the air surrounding her were scraping on raw nerves.

"Please stop, Katie." He crossed his arms over his chest and leaned back against the kitchen counter.

His pleading made her even more determined to push forward. "How can I come to grips with this knowing nothing?"

"Facts won't help." He dropped his head, staring past his folded arms to the floor.

"I'll find out. I'm a newspaper reporter. This is a compact little community."

"Don't pry. You'll disturb a lot of people."

She picked up a paper napkin and ripped it in half. What good had ever come from protecting Jeff's name? She glared at him. "How dare you be mysterious? I gave myself to you again. I have a right to know. I can't separate you from your behavior the way I used to try to."

"I'm going to take care of this." He walked past her to the stairs and a few minutes later she heard his car drive off.

She reached for the phone on the bar and called Maxine. Hearing Maxine's voice, rich and full as ever at the other end, made Katie double over in anguish but she managed to form the words: "We can't come. We're having an emergency here. I'm so sorry after all your plans and preparations."

"An emergency? You sound awful."

"You must know it's something bad to stop me from making this trip right now." Recalling how hiding other secrets had made her feel part owner of them and the guilt that came with them, Katie wouldn't hedge this time. Jeff deserved to own this one all by himself.

"If he's put a hand on you again, call your local sheriff now! Or I will."

"It's not that. I think I feel as badly though."

"Damn, Katie. After all the other shit, don't tell me he's fucking around now too?"

"Oh, yes," Katie said. *Oh my God. My God!* She bent over the sink. "Just when I'd forced myself trust him again."

"You must be dying. Shit! After giving him another chance. You want me to fly to Boston?"

"I don't know what I want. I only found out a few minutes ago." Her voice caught in her throat; she coughed and then swallowed. "We were doing well. I even finally put the divorce on hold last week. Why would he do this now?"

"Because he has brass balls, that's why. He's giving you the finger in a brand new way. I've been afraid ever since you got together with him again. Up his ass! I couldn't wait to see you. You go back to Boston now and cry your eyes out. Then come out here."

"Damn, Maxine. Why did I give him an opportunity to hurt me all over again? I haven't absorbed this. It isn't real yet but I'll call you before doing anything."

"If you don't call, I'm going to fly out there and make a scene he'll never forget."

Katie said goodbye but kept the receiver in her lap as if not restoring it to its base would save the California trip from being scrapped entirely. If only she'd never ever met him in the first place. She would gladly give up any sweet experiences with him, to prevent the pain she was having this minute. But why would he have a relapse now when he might be at the point of getting just what he has wanted?

The next morning Katie recognized Caroline Martin's voice, nasal and demanding on the phone and asking for Jeff. "He isn't here," Katie said. She had told him the night before to sleep in the guest house so had no idea where he had gone early that morning.

"Tell him I need for him to call me back right away."

Caroline Martin, licensed psychologist and busybody making herself indispensable to the community, exactly what Katie didn't need that very moment. The nerve of her calling Jeff at home with such a bossy tone anyway. There was something off balance about the behavior of this Stone Harbor princess. Sure, Jeff seemed to be seriously carving out a second VIP status for himself in this brand new community but why would he suddenly be using social worker psychobabble? Because he picked it up from this rude Dr. Martin, Katie thought now. Phrases like "giving too much" and "being a caretaker" would not have rolled smoothly off his tongue a few weeks ago. And, what about that book, *The Love Addiction: Breaking Co-Dependency?* Remembering how Jeff had whipped it from her hand as if it were a timed explosive, Katie slid off her bar stool and went down to the master bedroom.

Sweeping her hand across the nightstand shelf and finding nothing, she turned to Jeff's bureau and started to search one drawer at a time until in the bottom drawer she found the book hidden under a layer of jockey shorts. Rolling backwards onto the bed, Katie flipped open the book and stopped abruptly at the title page where a handwritten inscription read: "Dear Jeff, Don't give up. You will recover from your addiction.

Love, Caroline."

Ripping wildly through the rest of the pages, Katie scanned notations in the margins scribbled in the same pinched handwriting:

"Obsessed with Katie" – "Example of Katie's destructive love..."

Her eyes also traveled quickly over yellow ribbons streaming across text. She read whole paragraphs where Jeff's name had been inserted above the word "co-dependent".

Finally, dropping the book to the floor, she hugged a pillow tight to her middle and rocked back and forth. The women she had been conjuring up earlier as possible mistresses were nothing like Dr. Caroline Martin. None of them would have had personal conversations with Jeff; none would have analyzed his relationship with his wife. What had Jeff told Caroline Martin to bring her to the conclusions inscribed in this book? Did he actually believe what he told her? Katie lay back on the bed and buried her head in a pillow. She wished she had back one of the other women she'd envisioned earlier: a brunette over-permed floozy hanging out at the Drunken Whaler, a muscle-bound lap swimmer at the health club, a Farah Fawcett look-alike just about everywhere.

Chapter Sixteen

Katie stood up and flashed the book in front of Jeff. Before he could speak, she opened it and read aloud one of the underlined passages: "Participating in a triad relationship might be used by a co-dependent to put distance between himself and his dependent partner."

He walked past her and looked out at the ocean through the sliding glass doors. "I told you to leave it alone," he said.

No matter how painful, she wasn't going to let him pretend this out of existence like so many things in the past. "You said you'd learned to empathize with me. So look at me. How do you think I'm feeling?"

He turned around. "Look, I'm sorry. You weren't here. I was alone."

"As *I* was when you were away on all your business trips." She tossed the book onto an end table. Caroline Martin with her skullcap hairdo and fierce pale eyes still seemed miscast as a femme fatale to Katie, but she pressed on. "Does she sleep with married men often, or were you special?" Katie wound a handful of hair behind one ear; she kept on though her voice was trembling. "You have your own therapist. Why would you listen to Caroline Martin?"

"She's sympathetic. She understands my need to please you."

Need to please me? No, Katie wasn't about to listen to Caroline's eleventh hour analysis of their marriage. Instead, to believe any of this, she needed to picture the two of them together, as preposterous as that seemed to her. "So where did you and Caroline conduct these cozy chats where she gave you all this understanding?"

"The first time was in a coffee shop after a village council meeting. The following Saturday, she invited me to lunch at her place." He waved a hand in front of his face. "Don't do this. No more questions."

She had a right to ask questions, more right than he did to have a separate personal life now that she'd given him another chance to prove himself. "Talking is one thing. Why the rest?" she asked.

"Just happened."

The casualness of his answer silenced Katie for a moment. Getting her voice back, she asked, "Have you told Dr. Sherman about Caroline?"

"I haven't seen Dr. Sherman since meeting Caroline."

Katie sank into a nearby living room chair and clasped her hands together in her lap.

Jeff hadn't moved except to rest his shoulder against one of the glass doors. Seeing him silhouetted against the dusk and lowering sun on the water, this conversation seemed unreal. Katie knew all the words – affair, adultery, infidelity, and yet she had purposely pushed the act itself from her line of vision. She hadn't let herself see "the thing" taking place. Her questions ought to be taking more direct aim even if she choked on the answers. "Where did you and Dr. Martin conduct your infidelity? There aren't many motels to speak of nearby."

First producing a long sigh, he answered, "At Caroline's."

Katie winced hearing him use Caroline's name in this context. She could almost hear him addressing her: "Caroline this", "Caroline that". What else did he call her? Sweetheart? Babe? My girl? Yes, it was getting more real.

Jeff suddenly reeled around, crossed the living room and rushed downstairs to their bedroom.

To think I pitied Caroline that night in the restaurant Katie remembered, then tried to recall Jeff's reaction to his adulterous partner sitting two or three yards from them while he pretended not to know her. Had he seemed nervous? It struck her now that he must have been seething underneath, annoyed at the woman for showing up at the restaurant, sitting across from them, staring at Katie and calling attention to herself like that. For stepping out of the compartment Jeff had surely assigned her to by then. The tension that had gripped Caroline's award dinner was also making more sense now. An adultery wouldn't remain a secret for long in a little closed society like Stone Harbor. He and Caroline must have been seen together in public.

"Let it go," Jeff kept telling her the next week each time Katie asked another question. Without hard facts, she feared she would go on inventing scenes in her mind that may have never occurred, discarding them later only to substitute others. She couldn't let this slip into their old gray zone of half memories and unmentionable topics. No, she *wouldn't* stop. By pasting bits of the story together, she might create a whole picture, one that could help explain why Jeff had ripped apart what he had begged her to put back together. *At the very moment in fact when I was feeling invincible with my magazine on its way and a trip to San Francisco only days off. But, worst of all, just as I was struggling to revive old lost feelings for him.*

Katie wanted to run as far away from this place as possible, but she couldn't seem to leave having all her plans up in the air and no real understanding of what had happened. She moved aimlessly about the house; Christmas came and went. Jeff went to the gym; she drove to the market; they watched television hardly speaking; he slept in the guesthouse. A golf ball had lodged in her throat refusing to dissolve. Some of the hurt might have been diluted with tears, but her eyes stayed bone dry. She felt foolish and stupid for trying to hold that dried up old bouquet of dream flowers close again, trying to have its aroma intoxicate her one more time. She hadn't guessed, hadn't suspected that he was regressing. Damn him for being able to put up such a front!

At first, a bedraggled Jeff acted like a dog left out in the rain but gradually he grew more spirited. On New Year's Eve he came into the living room where Katie was sitting and announced, "I'm going to the New Year's party at the Boat Club."

She turned and saw that he was dressed in a dark suit, white shirt, gold cufflinks, black and white striped tie. Filled with rage, she countered, "We were supposed to be in California for New Year's Eve!"

"I know you're angry, Katie." He backed away from her and started to leave. "But I have to tell her in person that it's over. You and I have to try to get past this and talk about *us* again."

"At a celebration, dressed like a groom, you're going to have a heart to heart with her? Sure, why not?"

"I have to go. I promised her I would be there. People know she and I are friends. She would be humiliated if I didn't show up."

"And will anybody wonder where I am on New Year's Eve?"

"They won't ask," he said and hurried down the stairs.

She heard his car inching down the icy driveway. *I could trail after him to the party. Maybe offer a toast to my husband's mistress,* Katie fantasized. A moment later, envisioning herself actually doing this, she got up from her chair suddenly and bounced down the stairs. In the bedroom, she took out the black strap cocktail dress and a pair of black satin heels she'd planned to wear at Maxine's New Year's party in Berkeley. She got dressed, applied some blush and mascara and lipstick and brushed her long hair into a bun, fastening it at the back with a large gold clip. Then glancing quickly at the full length mirror, she pulled on her coat and ran from the house.

In the car she shivered and turned on the heater, then snapped on the radio and started her drive down the hill toward the Stone Harbor New Year's Eve party. She pulled up in front of the Boat Club and through its large bay windows had a clear view of exquisitely dressed guests chatting and sipping cocktails, others moving dreamily across the dance floor.

Suddenly, as if shaking herself loose from a horrendous nightmare, Katie jerked herself up in her driver's seat and gasped: *What grotesque thing was I about to do? Have I lost all of my pride?* Grasping the steering wheel with pinched fingers, she sped past the glittering lights of the spectacularly decorated boathouse. At the intersection of the coastal road and the expressway entrance, a sign read: "North – Boston – South – Stone Harbor." She hesitated, wiggling the steering wheel first left, then right, until a horn blast from her rear jolted her and she turned southward. Then she rationalized: *We are still legally married. Half of this home actually also belongs to me. Why should I be the one to vanish?*

Back at the house, she ripped off her coat, then ran to the bedroom and changed back into jeans and sweatshirt. Next she grabbed an open bottle of white wine from the refrigerator, filled a glass and drank half of it in one swallow. She gravitated from one clock to another checking the time for the next two hours. She hadn't let Jeff touch her since discovering his affair two weeks earlier, and yet imagining him talking with Caroline again, was making her damn mad.

She turned on the television and watched the ball drop to the roof of the Times Building in New York. Feeling as diminished by his adultery as by one of his explosions, Katie recalled, *I promised myself never to feel this way again.* She wanted Jeff to tell Caroline Martin that she and all her psycho-theories were shit. She went back to the kitchen and refilled her wine glass again.

She curled up to a gathering of pillows on the floor in front of the television and fell asleep until Jeff bounded up the stairs. "What time is it?" she asked looking up at him and shaking herself awake.

"One o'clock."

"It took you this long to accomplish your mission?"

"It's done," he said, reaching for her hand. "Sleep by yourself again if you like. But can we try to get back to normal tomorrow?"

Jeff spent most of New Year's Day shoveling another night's snow from the driveway and their private road. Katie believed if it were possible he would have shoveled his way up the coast to Canada to save himself from having to discuss the night before. She took a ham from a hot oven and set it on a cutting board. When Jeff came in finally, he made himself a sandwich and sat down across from her at the dining table. "The hood of your car got crunched last night. The windshield is busted," he said. "A deer must have come out of the woods and leaped at it."

The thought of her car being attacked in the night gave Katie a start; she fought an impulse to run from the kitchen to the car to investigate. Instead, she took another sip of tea. "Why would a deer do a thing like that? There were no lights to attract it or frighten it."

"Saw its own reflection in the windshield, maybe." He picked up his sandwich from his plate and concentrated on eating.

Alternative ways a windshield could get broken were playing themselves out in her head. Suddenly picturing Jeff's hand raising up a shovel and slamming it hard against the glass, she wondered if his encounter at the boathouse had gone bad. She drank the rest of her tea and tried to quiet herself. Tomorrow she would have to think of a more credible theory to replace the deer leaping through the windshield of a darkened, parked car story to tell the glass man at the garage.

Katie, guessing he wasn't going to give her a rundown on the New Year's Eve party, finally asked him outright, "What happened at the club last night?"

"I took care of the matter," he said and then finished the last of his sandwich. She kept her eyes on him and waited. With her staring him down, he added, "in a way that will let her save face. We have to treat their favorite daughter with kid gloves – if we want to have a proper place in this community, that is."

Katie got up and carried her cup to the sink. "Hard to save anybody's face at this point, isn't it? People in a small town are difficult to fool."

"I have their sympathy."

"Their sympathy?" She turned around. "Why would you have their sympathy? What did you tell people?"

Without answering, he got up from his chair and started toward the living room. She remembered how he had regularly twisted things to put blame on her; he could have said she was a hopeless druggie, a child molester, anything. If so, who could she possibly turn to in this village for help if necessary? Jeff had a way with people; they believed him.

She gazed out the kitchen windows. *How could I have allowed myself to suffer one more insult at his hands? And how could I reveal this latest idiocy to Natalie. And, oh, my God – to Steve.*

Alone in the house the next morning, Katie picked up the phone and asked Caroline, "And who shall I say is calling?"

"I think you know."

"You'll have to tell me."

"Put him on the phone or I'll..."

Katie yanked the cord from the wall jack, cutting off Caroline and then went out for a long drive. When she returned, Jeff had plugged in the phone again. She glared at him across the kitchen bar. "Why is she still calling? I thought you settled the matter. I'm going to report her to the phone company or the police." She had just thought of the latter, but it sounded like a good idea now.

Jeff hunched up his shoulders, holding his palms out in a gesture of hopelessness and left the room. What did that mean? "I don't care what you do?" "Don't do it?" "Have her booked if you like?"

Katie yearned to talk to Dr. Henry but was too embarrassed to call him. She hadn't seen him since moving from Barrington to Boston and at the time he'd expressed a strong opinion that she only encounter Jeff in a safe place for necessary business reasons. Why should Dr. Henry want to listen to this latest utter idiocy in her life?

Jeff finally slipped back into his old game of "let's pretend it never happened".

"I'm making dinner tonight," he said while hauling a bag of groceries into the kitchen and setting them on the counter. "Something special, one of your favorites."

"Is that right?" Katie answered, having lost all interest in eating food. *If he's hungry he can do the cooking. How could he screw around with another woman and expect me to act normal?* She didn't give a hoot what he was cooking up in the kitchen. She wanted to storm out of the house, drive over to

Dr. Caroline Martin's and kick in her door. Then spit in her face and set her house on fire.

Jeff turned around, looking perplexed. "I think you're losing weight. You don't have to talk to me, but eat something tonight." He took a skillet from a cabinet. "Okay, I'll call her again tomorrow and tell her to knock off the phone calls."

Furious, Katie gave him a long cold look. His vacation was almost over. In a few days he would be back at work in Barrington and she would be left to deal with Caroline on her own for a week. Katie wasn't going to walk away from this with her head hanging, but in truth, she had no idea how to handle Caroline. Who was she in any case? A lonely, desperate, pitiful woman? Or, a lady of entitlement, the village heroine who believed herself above reproach?

As Jeff concocted his dinner, Katie imagined a third alternative for himself. Against her own gun control principles, she would purchase a shotgun. If she had to use it, she would claim self-defense. Better yet, she would sling the weapon over her shoulder like a vigilante. Stroll down the village streets telling interested bystanders that she was gunning for the local psychiatric social worker. What could folks say? They couldn't call it a concealed weapon.

No, Katie was not about to be intimidated by a two-bit do-gooder with the morals of an alley cat. If Jeff didn't see the urgency here, she did. She was furious with both of them. First Jeff, but the alley cat, too.

"Jeff isn't here," Katie said not surprised to hear Caroline's throaty voice on the phone again the next morning. Caroline was not going to withdraw gracefully. "Don't ever call our home again!" Katie demanded.

"You should have stayed in Boston," Caroline snapped back.

"Stop calling here," Katie said.

Caroline waited a dramatic moment to respond to Katie's demand. "That's no longer your home. If you don't believe me, take a look at the top shelf of the cabinet over the stove. I put something there that might interest you."

I put something there. Katie hung up and lowered herself to a barstool. *She's been here, inside this home!* Hoping her legs wouldn't buckle on her, Katie got up, pulled a chair over to the kitchen counter and stood on it. Heart pounding, she reached into the top cabinet and dragged a spiral notebook out from behind a stack of bowls. She rushed over to the guesthouse, locked a bedroom door and dropped the notebook onto the bed. Then lowering herself to the mattress, she picked up the venomous evidence reluctantly, opened to the first page and began to read the small, pinched handwriting she recognized from the *Love Addiction* book: *"Katie, convincing herself that Jeff was violent, soon believed it. Katie was threatened by normal expressions of anger. Jeff sublimated his emotions to please her. He took good care of Katie while she showed little compassion for him."*

Katie dropped the notebook to the bed and held her head in her hands *My, how these conclusions of Caroline's must have pleased Jeff,* she thought, while scooping up the notebook again and flipping through page after page. Noting a gradual change in Caroline's tone, her language becoming more personal, her notes beginning to sound like entries in a diary rather than clinical evaluations. One special paragraph leaped up from the page and slapped Katie in the face: *"I feel at home here this morning. Had a shower. Grabbed a towel from a rack next to the vanity. Smelled Katie's perfume on the terrycloth. Light and airy, nothing to it. Took her robe from the closet and wore it. Put on her sweatshirt; jeans too small. Wore a pair of Jeff's jogging pants. Last night I slipped into one of her silk nightgowns. I belong in this house. Pretending to be pleased* with my previous life, I'd actually been waiting all this time for Jeff to arrive in Stone Harbor."

Starting to feel light headed, Katie leaned her head against the backboard. Now she was beginning to see Caroline as determined and willing to do anything to get what she wanted. Presently, Jeff. Even as a chill ripped across her neck and shoulders, Katie kept on reading: *"I threw a few of my things in the dryer...set the alarm...stretched out on the bed next to Jeff, rolled over and let my hand caress his arm and shoulder."*

Fighting for a breath, Katie read every word of the explicit language that followed. Jeff had dismissed the affair with three words saying, "It just happened". Then he had followed with, "This has nothing to do with you and me, Katie." Caroline's version, hot, damp and sensual, disputed Jeff's "just happened" explanation.

Katie read on as though powerless to stop. In Caroline's next entry, she was in Katie's kitchen preparing a surprise dinner for Jeff. Katie slapped the notebook closed. What kind of woman permits herself to enter another woman's home and bed and kitchen and then boasts about it? A bitter woman? Angry? Jealous? Katie ordered herself to stop trying to analyze Caroline or her possible motivations. She didn't want to empathize with Caroline. Period. Whatever Caroline's reasons or excuses, leaving this journal behind was a purposeful, cruel act.

Katie ran back to the main house still clutching the notebook. She stood in the doorway of the master bedroom waiting to get her bearings. Then plowing into the room, she dropped the notebook on the floor and dove at the bed. She ripped off all the lovely bedclothes she had personally chosen for this beautiful bed Jeff had ordered special from Finland. First shoving them into three large Hefty bags, she carried them outside and stuffed them into a trash can.

Back inside, she cleansed the mattress with a sponge and soap, wiped it with a clean cloth and sprayed it with disinfectant.

Then she scrubbed her sink and vanity, tossing her toothbrush and a bar of partly used soap into the wastebasket. Finished with that, she scoured the adjoining bathtub and shower stall. Whipping towels from the rods and racing to the laundry room, she shoved them into the washer, then came back and sprayed all the bathroom tile surfaces with Lysol. Grabbing a can of wood soap and a small pail from the broom closet, she swabbed the tops of her dresser and Jeff's bureau and both nightstands. She plucked unfamiliar magazines from the nightstand shelves and dropped them into another Hefty bag.

With one load of laundry going, she ran upstairs and scoured the kitchen appliances and counters and dropped utensils and dishes from the cabinets into the dishwasher. She lowered herself to a barstool to catch her breath but her gaze drifted over to her coffee maker. Rising up again, she grabbed the carafe by the handle and shoved it under the faucet. Next, remembering her old cookbooks, most of them from her Pacific Heights flat, that she kept on a shelf above the sink, she screamed: "Her fingerprints are everywhere. She's pawed everything in the house!"

She held a finger to each temple. Her thoughts still playing leapfrog from one grim possibility to the other, she ran back downstairs, picked up the notebook from the floor and took it upstairs. She turned to the last page, some inner voice telling her that the final entry would be dated December 15. She dropped back onto a stool and read: *"November 27. Went to bed early last night. I have to leave for appointments after breakfast. I heard Jeff on the phone making reservations at the Atlantic House for dinner tonight. Could Katie be returning from Boston? Surely not for long. I'm sure."*

Katie slid off her stool, went out to the deck and swallowed mouthfuls of cold January air. She had been too exhilarated that night at the restaurant to mind Caroline's stares from another table. Afterward, she and Jeff had come home from their celebration dinner and made love in the bed where he and Caroline had been that morning, where all of the scents had intermingled, Jeff's and Caroline's, Katie's and Jeff's, Caroline's and Katie's. Katie tugged at her sweatshirt where cold perspiration dripped down between her breasts.

She turned around on the deck and glanced back into the house, the living room, the kitchen, the stairs down to the bedroom. This beautiful home was turning on her like a dark wind coming at her from behind, forming a grand swell that was swallowing her up in its wash. If the sailboat were in the water, Katie would motor out to it, spend the night, smell the salt air and feel the comforting motion of the V-berth under her. She grasped the deck rail again and took another swallow of brittle air. Hadn't Jeff taken the boat out once more while she was in Boston? Oh, God, had Caroline been with him? Had she laid her naked body in their precious V-berth, contaminating that last bit of their private space? Remembering her own summer clothes in a locker on the port side, her toiletries in the cabinet in the head, Katie imagined Caroline's hands and moist perspiration smeared all over her belongings.

How could you let this happen, Jeff? How ill are you? She came in from the deck, went down to the master bathroom and held a wet washcloth to her face. With the other hand, she pulled open the top drawer of her vanity and picked up her douche bag between two fingers. She dropped it into the wastebasket, straightened up and caught sight of herself in the mirror, eyes with the look of a hunted animal listening to the howling dogs getting closer.

Chapter Seventeen

Jeff strolled into the kitchen, grabbed a Coke from the refrigerator, opened it and took a long drink.

Katie sat down on a stool and, glaring across the bar at him, spat out her words: "My God. That woman was inside this home!"

He plunked down the Coke bottle on the counter. "I told you to get a grip. Can we possibly get our lives back on track soon?"

"With a new bombshell every day?"

He folded his arms across his chest and shook his head back and forth.

Lifting the notebook from her lap, Katie slapped it onto the counter. "You didn't know about her journal?"

A band of crimson crept slowly up his neck; his shoulders stiffened, one hand gripped the edge of the kitchen cabinet. Biting his lip, he wrapped the other hand tight around the Coke bottle. He glanced out the kitchen window for a moment, then set the bottle back onto the kitchen counter releasing it slowly.

Noting that the bottle was no longer a potential missile, Katie exhaled and slumped back in her stool.

"I wish this hadn't happened," he mumbled.

"But you couldn't resist Caroline's words that soothed you so? Even if they cancelled everything you had learned with Dr. Sherman? All those astute insights that allowed me to try again." Katie smacked the notebook hard with the palm of her hand. "I feel stupid. I thought you were happy."

He walked over to her and lifted her hand from the journal. "I was happy until you started to spend so much time on that magazine."

Thinking she might get sick with his fingers wrapped around hers, Katie swung herself off of the stool and darted into the living room. "I can't think straight now that I'm mired in your affair."

Jeff walked toward her holding out his arms.

Quickly backing away from him, she said, "I'm going to throw out that bed. I trashed the bedclothes and scrubbed the mattress and headboard. But that bed will never, never be clean again! Fuck you! That woman used my vanity, my towels, my robe. My nightgown. My nightgown, Jeff! For God's sake!"

He swung around and slapped his hand hard against a bookcase shelf, knocking books to the floor. "I want you and Caroline to both settle down. That's all I want. Everybody to calm down."

Katie studied his face from across the room, that face that had hidden one more secret as his outstretched arms had welcomed her return from Boston two weeks earlier. "Calm down? Face it, Jeff. You're in over your head this time. Your old walls of demarcation are crumbling. People aren't staying in the compartments you've assigned them to."

But before she finished her sentence Jeff had already swung around and started toward the stairs. "I'm going out for a ride to let you cool down," he said.

* * * * * * *

The next day Katie's mind leaped from one possible plan of action to the other while Jeff was out of the house. Sensing his heightened aggravation, she couldn't chance another confrontation with him. She would have to make a move. But that very moment Caroline called again and Katie hung up without saying a word. Then she yanked on her jacket and scooped up her car keys.

Outside she skidded across a layer of crusty snow to her car. A mile past Stone Harbor village, she turned down a narrow road marked Spring Drive to an address she'd found earlier in Jeff's phone book. Spotting a mailbox bearing Caroline's name, she parked directly in front of her country home clothed in a web of brown winter vines. Just then, Caroline, decked out in a cashmere wool suit, high-heeled boots and a floppy knit hat, exited her front door.

Katie leaped from her car door and walked briskly up a stone path toward Caroline.

"You have no right to be here," Caroline shouted. "You're trespassing."

Katie gasped, stopping short a few feet from Caroline. "You ought to know. You're the expert on trespassing!"

With unblinking eyes peeled on Katie, Caroline yanked her shoulder purse into place. "You're forgetting something." She threw her shoulders back. "Jeff invited me into his home."

"*Legally our* home. We *are* married," Katie snapped back. At the same time she noted that Caroline's throaty voice had lost some of its fiber and it occurred to Katie that Caroline may have expected her to be shattered by the notebook. "How low can you sink?" she asked Caroline. "My underpants were in the clothes hamper. My clothes were hanging in an open closet in full view of the bed. If a woman is away, do you think her husband and the home are fair game? You have no morals! Or, did you think you could be the perfect Katie Jeff longed for? What a shame you wanted to take over my life, knowing so little about it, or about Jeff. You are disgusting!" Katie took in a quick breath. "I wanted to tell you that in person."

"He's tired of taking care of you." Caroline picked at the slicked down blonde hair framing her face under her hat. "That much I know." She tossed her head back and her purse strap slipped. She caught it and slapped it back onto her shoulder.

"Taking care of me? You are really on the wrong track if you believe that." Katie shrugged her shoulders. "No more phone calls. That's an order. You call again and I'll have an attorney ready to sue your behind for harassment."

Caroline laughed. "Harassment? I can call Jeff any time I like. You've already lost him. If you had any sense you would realize that." She sneered. "You believe you can sue me in my home town? I know how cruelly you treated Jeff's children and how you abandoned him when he needed you most. And so do most of the Stone Harbor townspeople by now. Sure, sue me. Then I can chase your butt back to Boston for good."

"Good Lord, woman. I could expose you and your adulterous self in a court of law. And sue you for slander. How would that be for your reputation? And guess what? I too have friends in Rhode Island."

"Jeff would stand by me no matter what. He's a good man and he deserves better. He needs me."

"You poor woman, sitting here in these idyllic surroundings waiting for Prince Charming and along came Jeff. He has won you over, hasn't he? What a bill of goods he must have sold you! Strange though, shouldn't you have seen through his motives better than any of us? Aren't you supposed to be a mental health professional?"

"Which is why I understand him and why I've been able to help him."

"I'm pissed enough to tell you to go screw yourself and a lot more. But I see that it would be pointless," Katie said, then paused, and feeling she'd expressed herself adequately, told Caroline, "My advice to you is to get out now and save yourself a lot more trouble. I guess there's not much chance of that happening, is there?"

"None at all," Caroline said. "I won't desert Jeff the way you did."

Nevertheless feeling satisfied, almost triumphant, Katie whirled around. Then over her shoulder, she waved her hand above her head. As she marched back to her car she could have sworn she heard bugles trumpeting her exit.

On the drive home, feeling almost giddy, Katie asked herself: *Whatever am I doing in this picture postcard village having it out with a delusional woman who's been sneaking in and out of my bedroom?* Then Katie started to giggle hysterically. How unreal it all seemed suddenly. Or, was it so real she had to put emotional distance between herself and Jeff's outrageous mess quickly?

She stared ahead at the road. She grinned and laughed again asking herself – who knows what might happen next? Caroline could have a change of heart. Jeff could find a conscience. Sure they could. The improbability of these things occurring sent her reeling once more. For whatever this confrontation might not change, it had cheered her up for a few minutes and that seemed to make it worthwhile.

Bounding up the stairs to the living room Katie announced to Jeff, "I took care of matters myself."

He glanced up from an open magazine on the bar, half listening.

"I drove over to her house and told her to stop harassing us."

"You what?" He bounced up from his stool. "You can't attack one of their own."

"I didn't attack her. I told her to stop calling us."

Jeff roared, "Caroline wields power in Stone Harbor. You don't know a damn thing about getting along with people."

"I do just fine with people. She is not going to insert herself into my life another day."

"Damn, Katie. You're too open and frank. These people were getting ready to appoint me to the village council. I was negotiating to open a small branch office of International in Stone Harbor. You didn't know that, did you? If there's one thing I'm aware of, it's how to get accepted somewhere. Once you're embraced by community leaders in a place like this, you can do no wrong. But, rub them the wrong way, and you can do no right. There will be no stopping her if she's pissed."

"You're right, Jeff. Look out the window. She has sent the cavalry after us. The horse brigade is already ascending the hill. They'll be drumming us out of town by nightfall." Katie sank onto a stool at the other end of the bar. "I can't believe you're upset about your position in this sleepy little enclave. And what makes you think these good people will embrace you now after you've violated their golden-haired daughter?"

Jeff's eyes darted here and there; he wasn't listening to her. Did he really believe his life would be serene again if he could save his image in Stone Harbor? Katie was astounded at how much that seemed to mean to him. She hadn't noticed his need for that kind of recognition in Barrington. The subject never came up, but then, as a business leader there, she admitted, Jeff had been assured of VIP status from the start.

He got up and paced the kitchen, took out a bottle of ice water from the refrigerator and, shoving the door shut, rattled glass jars inside. Lips pinched, he warned Katie, "Stay out of it from now on. Don't make a move. Don't answer the telephone."

Realizing that his frustration was escalating, Katie lowered her voice. "I drew on all my emotional resources to try to start over with you. This home represented hope for trying to begin anew. I thought we were becoming real friends."

He dashed around the bar, then stopped. "Tell you what. I'll call Caroline from the gym tonight and settle this once and for all." He reeled around, left the room and ran down the stairs.

From the solarium windows Katie watched his car speed away. In the silence that followed, she turned and gazed out the sliding glass doors toward the bay where the last of the day's sunlight shimmered on quiet waters. She glanced back at the home. Still standing.

Might this herald the end of Caroline? Might Jeff return to his own therapist? She sighed thinking – sure, with the assistance of a certified miracle maybe. "A miracle is just a wish that comes true," she had whispered to Marijo in the dark of their third story bedroom a long time ago, and Marijo had scoffed at her childish sister. But Katie had believed in miracles back then.

Katie started down the coastal highway while continuing to invent absurd reasons for Jeff not returning from the gym on time. He could have stopped at the grocery store; he could have stopped for gas. She didn't know exactly why she was looking for him, except that she'd be damned if she was going to be lied to one more time.

Driving past Stone Harbor and turning onto Spring Road, she parked across the street from the scene of her afternoon's confrontation and gazed numbly at Jeff's car in Caroline's driveway without emotion as if viewing a still photograph, little birds stopped in flight, fluffy clouds unmoving.

She restarted the engine and headed back to the highway.

* * * * * * *

Tossing her car keys on the bar quickly she tried to plan her next move but just then Jeff threw open the front door. Taking two steps at time he bounded up the stairs yelling, "Katie! All's well." He blasted into the living room. "I got her on the phone...."

"I saw your car in her driveway," Katie said calmly, no tremor in her voice.

"Damn it, Katie. You shouldn't have driven over there. I decided I had to talk to her in person. And it worked this time. She's being agreeable now."

"Quite a change from a few hours ago. How agreeable was she?"

"I smoothed her ruffled feathers, you might say."

Katie listened, almost intrigued as if she'd constructed a protective wall around herself while waiting patiently for him to elaborate.

"Believe me, if Caroline carried a grudge, she could cook our goose around here," he said.

"Are you crazy, Jeff? You don't think it's charred to a crisp already?"

"Don't worry; I have these Yankees solidly in my corner."

"Oh, yes. I understand you made *me* the villain, abandoning you, being cruel to your kids. They think I'm the one who should be run out of town. Maybe I'll sue both you and Caroline for slander."

Not expecting an answer, she sat down on a stool and watched him pace back and forth in the kitchen. "You made fun of the bluebloods in Barrington," she said.

"I didn't need them there. I sure don't take them seriously here either. You work with what you have. If Caroline doesn't lose complete respect for me, she'll be useful."

"She's losing respect for you?"

"She says I'm caving in to you."

"Being my caretaker again?"

Jeff nodded. "Probably."

"So, would a loving caretaker ever be violent with the person he's caretaking? I mean in Caroline's professional opinion?"

"Caroline doesn't think I'm a monster. I was never as bad as you and Dr. Sherman painted me. She understands my temperament better than either of you."

"Good God! Caroline never had to walk around the debris from one of your rampages. Sure as hell, she never had to run from the house in the dark of night." Katie took a long slow breath. "Wake up, Jeff. You and I both know why I left you. And we both know I only came back because Dr. Sherman told me you had learned to control your anger."

His lips stretched thin. "I didn't intend to have an affair. I needed some understanding."

"Understanding, Jeff? Damn! So has this affair made you feel better about yourself?" Her mocking tone was foolhardy at this point, but she couldn't seem to stop herself.

He rolled his eyes. "No righteousness, please."

Her anger was going to kill her if she didn't let go of it. "Go to hell!" she blurted out. "We ordered that beautiful bed from Finland. Remember the night we christened it?"

She took in another big breath. "Stand still and listen to me! What if I met a man in Stone Harbor and brought him here when you were away and made intimate confessions to him about us? Then invited him to join me in our glorious bed to participate in passionate love-making with me? And then let him wear your robe and use your shaving lotion and dry himself with your bath towels? And cook in our kitchen and sit in your chair and nap on your sofa? How would you like that?" She looked away and forced herself to shut up while she was still able to because she was going to be screaming in another second and he wouldn't stand for that.

"Quit this," he yelled with a familiar sharp edge to his voice. "You would never do that! Jesus, Katie. We'll get back to where we were before this setback. I promise you."

For one second, from habit, she could *almost* feel herself sliding back into those dark waters. Thinking maybe there had been *some* exaggeration on her part, maybe there could be *some* working this out. But she grabbed hold of an imaginary branch of an imaginary tree at the water's edge, dug her fingers into it, and hung on. Over her shoulder she saw the accumulation of failed attempts to minimize terrible things and broken promises floating past her on the surface like so much toxic waste. Realizing she had not succumbed to old habits, she took a deep breath and forced her heartbeat to slow down.

"Don't tell me how to do this, Katie. I have to handle it my way."

"Your way created this. People aren't staying in their proper little containers according to your plans anymore."

"I don't know what the hell you're talking about half the time, Katie. Caroline's softening up. I know how to handle people."

"Is that so?" She turned away slowly and started down the stairs. Sitting at the side of the bed, she held onto herself, arm over arm as an image of Jeff and Caroline together in this very bed passed before her, blindsiding her and producing a blast of white anger too intense to be eased away by his sweet words *this time*. His body next to hers couldn't numb the pain as it used to. She got up from the bed and climbed the stairs back to the living room. "Caroline got to play house in this home and now she thinks she belongs here. And if I don't get out of here, I'll become a permanent player too in all this debauchery." She paused a moment, staring at him. "What the devil have you done, Jeff?"

The look she knew too well, complexion shiny and bright, delicate pattern of tiny veins drawing patterns on his cheeks, stiffening arm muscles, sent her quickly to the bar. She snatched up her car keys and made a dash for the stairs.

Jeff sprang forward and dashed after her shouting, "You aren't going to leave! You already found out we can't be apart.

You would only bounce back to me again. So sit back down. I've negotiated a peace accord with Caroline."

Katie raced out the front door and on to her car. Hearing him fast behind her on the path, she dove into the driver's seat, slammed the door and snapped the lock. "Katie! Don't!" he yelled, his hands splayed on her driver's side window.

She smashed her foot on the accelerator, backed up and turned forward into the driveway. He chased after her. Through the rear-view mirror, she watched him, his face a brilliant ruby color now as he came to a stop at the end of the highway, legs apart, shoes planted firmly on the snow covered gravel, hands clenched into tight fists at his sides.

Chapter Eighteen

"Katie, you shouldn't have left last night," Jeff sputtered. "I called Caroline after you left. She has backed off for good."

Though jolted awake by the telephone Katie was relieved to find herself back in her Boston condo. She dragged the phone into bed with her and pulled a quilt back over her head. "And so?"

"So I know what I have to do now to be the husband you want."

"Such as?"

"To start with, I'm going to see a realtor about selling the captain's house. And then, I'm going to let you get back to work on another issue of your periodical. In peace this time. By the way, that captain's house is a scary place when you're there alone. Did you ever notice how those pine trees out back have grown since we bought the place? Completely cover the kitchen window now. Can't see a damn thing out of it."

Katie smiled, figuring she'd escaped that ghost house just in time. Only recently she'd noticed a scraggly baby growth sprouting up from the snow in back of the Stone Harbor house. Perhaps trouble can reseed itself, dig in and take root in a brand new place, she wondered, sinking further into her quilt and pulling it tighter around her body.

"Anyway, that empty house is giving me the creeps," Jeff said. "The rooms seem to be closing in on me. I couldn't breathe the other night when I had to stay overnight in Barrington. I had to go outside to get some air in my lungs. I'm going to rent a suite of rooms to use the next time I have to stay overnight in Barrington. By the way, I talked to Tommy last night. The kids are all back from California and want to visit us in Stone Harbor for a weekend soon. They still need us, Katie."

"I'm going to stay in Boston," she said. "I'll contact the kids myself. That's all I want to say now." Even if she had further plans, she wouldn't have revealed them to him. And if he didn't hang up now, she would hang up first.

"Okay," he said. "I'll call tomorrow."

Wrapping the quilt around her shoulders, she dragged it behind her to the living room and sat down on the sofa. Well Jeff had gotten the bounce back in his voice, no doubt believing he'd convinced Caroline to lay low and thinking he could talk his Katie into working things out again. Katie pictured Jeff's twelve-year-old self, the child who could study a gang of boys in a new neighborhood and figure out what they were missing, supply it and win them over. The boy, who by junior high, could get himself accepted anywhere by anybody he desired.

Like the man, she realized with a start, who had just told her: "I know what I have to do to be the kind of husband you want."

What if, she asked herself, he had *never* believed in any of those changes she'd seen in him a year ago? And he was only offering her what he thought she needed in order to take him back?

Restless, Katie wandered room to room all day, these same questions dogging her into evening. Growing in importance, their answers seemed pivotal to understanding the rest, from the beginning perhaps. Finally, she reached for the phone, frantic to put her theory to him directly, even if he couldn't respond honestly.

"O'Connell residence," a woman's deep nasal voice answered and in a flash Katie pictured Caroline, her eager fingers grasping their bar telephone, ample bottom planted on a stool, a stool, as a matter of fact, that Katie had painted almond white to match the decorator kitchen cabinets last summer. *She is now removing garments from my closet and dresser drawers again,* Katie envisioned, *wearing whatever fits her, using my soaps and face cream and washcloths and towels. Stamping her fingerprints on my furniture, leaving her body imprints in our bed. Jeff is there, telling himself he's in control. Maybe even still believing it.*

She slipped the phone back in its cradle, turned down the answering machine volume and crawled back into bed. She rolled herself into the quilt again and stayed there most of the day and that night until the following morning.

When she got up finally she went back to the living room and pressed the call button on the answering machine. "Miss you and love you," Jeff assured her and then asked why she hadn't answered his calls.

I'm in closer touch with reality than either Jeff or Caroline, she realized, Jeff playing hopscotch in and out of other people's lives; Caroline losing herself in a private fantasy, preferring a stolen life to her own; Jeff, still convinced with a nudge here and there, that he can keep Caroline in his corner and Katie in his life.

She hit the erase button and sank into a living room chair, then glanced at a recent picture of Jeff and her last summer that sat on a nearby end table – morning sunlight on their faces. Beyond the scope of the camera, fog would have been rising from the ocean, hazy black dots transforming themselves into clusters of small rocky islands, white caps peaking and ebbing in the dark waters out at sea, sunrays filtering through their bedroom blinds, yellow slivers slipping across their bed. Katie reached over and slapped the picture face down on the table. How foolish she'd been to endow that new home with so much power, believing it capable of bringing lost love back to life.

Before changing her mind, Katie picked up her telephone and dialed Steve's private number at the *Gazette*. She had no expectations that Steve would want to hear from her. He'd been so proud of how well she was recovering during her separation from Jeff and so disturbed when she felt compelled to give Jeff a second chance.

She went speechless for a moment upon hearing Steve's voice again. "Hello? Hello?" he asked.

"Steve? It's Katie."

"Katie. My God!"

"I'm in Boston. Awful things have been happening. I'm sorry I let you down so. I'd like to talk to you if you can bear to even look at me again. I won't blame you if you can't."

After a slight hesitation, he said, "Where and when?"

"Later this afternoon if you can. About four o'clock at the First Stop Diner. Natalie too, if possible."

"I'll be there."

Then, longing to see Dr. Henry's unruly hair and rumpled suit and hear his steady voice again, Katie overrode her shame and called him. Yes, he said he would squeeze her into a half-an-hour appointment between two other patients that afternoon.

With good reason to leave her apartment, Katie felt a small surge of energy, enough to shower and dress for the first time in three days.

Their old family therapist came around his desk to welcome Katie, and then sat in a chair next to her. She gave him a rushed account of events in Stone Harbor and then buried her face in her hands. "I had to get out of there. He was back in the driver's seat. And I knew he was ready to explode again."

Dr. Henry leaned toward her, paused a moment and said, "This affair was punishment for you, the same as his rampages were. Both were meant to frighten you into doing what he wanted."

Katie clasped her hands together in her lap. "Jeff was bored while I was working in Boston, but I never suspected..." She put a fist to her forehead. "I should never have had anything to do with him again. I should have known better." She ran her fingers through her hair. "I've done a lot of thinking, hard thinking, during the past three days. I think I've always worked too hard at trying to make people love me. My father ignored me – still I tried and tried harder to win him over. Jeff became violent and even then I didn't give up on him. Strange, I was always afraid Jeff would leave me, rather than the other way around."

She crossed her arms and held herself tight at her waist. "With Jeff, I was scared about something all the time."

"You had nothing to do with your father's inability to express his emotions. And Jeff couldn't really love you as he should have because he's not a loving person. He doesn't know how to love. By the way, Katie, this always gave him a great advantage over you. He believed you would always stick by him, no matter what. And that you would come back to him whatever he did. He probably still believes this."

Dr. Henry peered at her over the top of his heavy horn rim glasses. "I can help you come to terms with all of this, but I would insist on one rule. For a change and for the most part, we are going to talk about you, not Jeff. Do you think you can do that?"

"Jeff would think I was being self-centered." She smiled. "Sorry. I'll try."

Steve met her at the entrance to the First Stop Diner. "Natalie called you again and again in Boston after you were supposed to have returned from California. You had her frantic."

Katie slid into the booth next to Natalie and across from Steve as Natalie held a finger up to a waitress to bring another coffee.

"I didn't go to California," Katie said before they could ask about the trip. It was time to forego pride in the name of honesty once more with her dear neglected friends.

After hearing Katie's account of what had happened in Stone Harbor, Natalie sputtered, "Disgusting! Horrific! Hell! We should have tied you to a bedpost to stop you from seeing him ever again. Ever! I mean ever!"

Steve had been tracing an invisible circle on the tabletop with his finger throughout Katie's report. "The man is sadistic," he said finally. "Fuck! I'd enjoy driving up there and throwing a torch to that goddam gorgeous house with him in it."

Katie could hardly bear to look at Steve knowing how she had disappointed and hurt him. "Thanks," she said, trying to hold back the tears welling up in her eyes.

"Say you're not going back to Stone Harbor for any reason," Natalie said. "For any reason!"

"I'm not even answering my phone."

Steve exhaled a long breath that sounded as if he'd been holding it in for months. "Good, we'll let your phone ring once and hang up, so you'll know it's us and then we'll call back."

Natalie reached into her purse, took out a cigarette and lit it. "Damn. He's found a new form of torture, hasn't he?"

"I thought you gave those up," Katie said.

"I did. This is what you do to me." Natalie inhaled her cigarette and blew smoke away from the booth. "A lot has happened at the paper. You can come back, you know." She took another drag.

Katie finally let herself look directly at Steve and linger there a moment. She was grateful that he'd decided to speak to her. "Any permanent changes in your life, Steve?" she asked, then wondered how she would feel if he said he was completely in love with a brand new woman.

"No permanent change," he said, emphasizing the word "permanent".

"Actually, I've been spending more time on my novel. Planning a trip to Europe soon, too."

"Great," Katie said, grateful for some positive news. "Please say you'll finally let me read your manuscript."

"Okay. When it's ready for critique," he said. "By the way, I read your first issue of *Moving On*. It was as good as I'd expected it to be." He paused. "Even without my editing help at the end." He tilted his coffee mug in her direction. "Congratulations." He set down the mug, reached across the table and clamped a hand over one of her hands.

Natalie snuffed out her cigarette. "A few drags, that's all I needed."

"How about you and Nathan?" Katie asked her.

"He's stopped pestering me about his moving to Rhode Island." Natalie chuckled pleasantly. "Truth is, we both like things as they are. For now, at least." She shoved one arm, then the other, into her coat sleeves. "Sorry, we have to get back to work, Katie. Are you positive you'll be okay in Boston? You can always stay with me if you don't want to be alone right now."

"Thanks, but I want to try to cope one hour at a time all by myself. It's been such a hellish nightmare. Can I see either or both of you after my appointment with Dr. Henry next Friday?"

Steve got up, then bent over and wrapped both arms around Katie's shoulders. "Sure. I'm just glad you're safe again."

Chapter Nineteen

Katie gazed out at Boston Harbor where daylight was beginning to fade and the outer harbor was bustling with traffic. Large cargo vessels and small pleasure boats were following one another toward the inner harbor in search of moorings and places to anchor or a berth before nightfall. Soon their crews would be lighting stoves to take the chill off cabins and reminiscing about their day long or month long voyages, as *Jeff and I used to do*, she remembered with mixed feelings. Foolish nostalgia in any case at this point, she realized. Instead she recalled events of the past few weeks – her helpful talks with Dr. Henry, encouraging responses from readers of the first issue of *Moving On* and lunches with loyal friends Steve and Natalie.

Catching a glimpse of herself in her bedroom mirror, faded jeans, ratty sweatshirt, limp hair, a few minutes later, she yanked open a bureau drawer and took out a bright green sweater and a clean pair of jeans. Stepping out of a steamy shower, she dressed, blow-dried her hair and applied a touch of pink to her lips. Feeling refreshed, she decided to walk over to Hanover Street in the old North End for a late afternoon cappuccino and afterward to browse through a local bookstore.

She pulled on her parka, swung open her condo door and then, stunned, stopped short finding herself face to face with Jeff. Appalled at the overall change in him in a few weeks, his gray pallor, face unshaven, clothes disheveled, she backed up three or four steps. "Jeff, what are you doing here?" she gasped. "How did you get by the security guard?"

Without answering, he stepped around her and into the condo. Once inside, he paced back and forth on the bare hardwood floors for a few seconds and then made a dash for the kitchen. He ran a glass of water and gulped it down and then came back to the living room and peered at Katie through dull, watery eyes. "How could I have fucked up so badly?" he asked.

"Sit down," she said to stabilize him and think what the hell to do next.

He lowered himself to the sofa. "We've had our troubles, but we've had beautiful times, too, haven't we?"

Katie nodded yes while trying to gage whether she could make it past him to the hall if she had to.

"I've never loved anyone but you," he said rubbing his eyes with the balls of his hands. When he lifted his head he looked worse than before, eyes sunken, pink at the edges, skin drawn.

"I could use a drink," he said.

"I have some Scotch," she answered, then moved cautiously past him toward the kitchen. Hands trembling, she reached for a bottle inside a cabinet, dropped ice cubes into a glass and poured Scotch over them. Still trying to absorb the shock of his arrival, she went back to the living room, handed him the drink and sat in a chair facing him but near the door.

"I don't know what I'd have done if you hadn't been here," he said setting his drink on the coffee table in front him. He wiped his forehead with the back of his hand. When he picked up his glass his hand shook; beads of Scotch spilled onto his jacket. He brushed over the damp spots with his sleeve. "I was happy. You were happy." He lifted his glass again dripping more Scotch onto his jacket, ignoring it this time.

If it weren't for the fear that was fast consuming her, she might have been sorry for him and his sudden pathetic appearance. All he ever wanted was for everyone to accept him at face value, never mind that it was the face he surmised they needed at the time. *Poor Jeff. He'd actually been selling himself all his life,* she realized now, *promising a potion for every ailment, strengthening it, weakening it, sweetening it, to fit someone's present need, whatever that was. Improvising, choreographing the dance, juggling all those balls. He'd even conjured up a pretend recovery to please his own approving psychiatrist.* She imagined herself reaching over, as usual, to brush his hair back from his forehead and help him sort it all out. Quickly, though, she fought this involuntary urge, asking instead a more urgent question. "Why are you here, Jeff?"

"To tell you I love you. And that everything's back to normal. You and I can go on now as if the past weeks never happened."

"Oh, really?" Katie stood up and moved slowly a few feet toward the door, but then realized if she tried to leave, he would catch up with her before she reached the elevator at the end of the hall. She glanced over at him. "What has changed, Jeff?"

"She's gone. Caroline's gone. That's what's different." He swallowed the rest of his drink. "I came to ask you to fly to the Bahamas with me."

"When?"

"Tomorrow. We could lay in the sun and have fun making up," he said. Then he bounded up from the sofa and sprinted across the room toward her. "Come on, Katie, have a drink with me," he said. Grasping her hand firmly he pulled her up from her chair and led her down the hall to the kitchen where he asked her to refill his drink and to make one for herself.

Deciding it was best to follow his orders for the moment, she reached for the ice container on the counter, shook some cubes into his glass and refilled it. She dropped a few cubes in another glass, poured a little Scotch over them and picked up the drink.

"That a girl," Jeff said, clinking his glass against hers. "Here's to us." Then he swung an arm around her shoulder and dragged her closer to him.

Taking hold of his hand at her back, she slid it around and led him down the hall. "Let's just sit in the living room and talk awhile," she said.

As he slid down onto the sofa she eased away from him and went back over to her chair.

"Come over here right now," he said patting the sofa seat next to him. "I want you here by my side."

"I think we should catch up a little. It's been so long. And shouldn't we be making plans for the trip to the Bahamas?" *Where was she going with this? God. Now he's going to get drunk. This isn't like him. I don't know what to expect from him if he's drunk.* She drew in a deep breath. *Maybe he'll pass out if he keeps drinking, but maybe not.*

"The Stone Harbor house is locked up tight. No reason we can't leave tomorrow. You'll love the Bahamas," he said. "We really need to put our troubles behind us." With one gulp he swallowed his new drink and gazed down at the empty glass. "I have an idea," he said. "Why not get the Scotch bottle and bring it in here.'

She rushed out to the kitchen, grabbed the bottle, hurried back to the living room and set it on the coffee table. Then she scurried over to her chair again.

Slurring his words slightly now, he said, "I may have to come over *there* if you won't join me here. We have our lives back, Katie." He poured more whiskey into his glass, drank it and raised his glass to her again. "Let's celebrate."

She lifted her glass in return. "Good for you, Jeff. So you finally got rid of Caroline."

"I promised I would, didn't I? Just think, here we are, the two of us again. I knew you'd be here waiting for me." He set down his glass and shifted himself on the sofa. Seeming desperate to say something more, he started twice, then stopped and unzipped his windbreaker jacket half way down again.

"What brought you here tonight, Jeff? Anymore than last week or next week?" she asked him. *Keep him talking until he passes out, or, please God, until I hear people in the hallway returning from work. And then I can make a run for it.*

He blew her a kiss. "Because I couldn't wait another day to see you. That's why I came today."

Feeling more desperate now, Katie said, "Instead of leaving for the Bahamas tomorrow, we could go out to the parking lot and get in your car and drive to the Stone Harbor home this minute. That would give us some time alone." *Say yes so we can get out of here and locate the security guard. And I can send you on your way.*

"Look at me. I'm in no shape to drive anywhere tonight."

With her mind racing now, Katie changed tactics. "Maybe you're right. Instead we should take a cab straight to Logan Airport. We could leave from Boston and be in New York tonight in time to take the next flight to the Bahamas."

"No, I want to stay here with you tonight. I can't wait to get you snuggled up to me again."

Responding fast, Katie said, "*I* can drive tonight. We can be at the Stone Harbor house in a few hours, spend the night there together and leave instead from Providence Airport in the morning." She forced herself to smile. "Let's leave now, Jeff."

"I don't think so," he said, then looked up and frowned. "You know what, Katie? It hasn't been easy for me since you left." With the ice in his drink melted, he took a swallow of watery Scotch. "For one thing, Caroline came to the house first thing the morning after you left Stone Harbor. I told her to leave, of course."

"But she stayed anyway." Katie said.

His head snapped up from his glass. "You knew that?"

"I called the house later that same evening and Caroline answered." Katie was glad to let him know that she hadn't been completely uninformed since returning to Boston.

"That's why you haven't answered my calls." He fingered his glass and then rubbed the back of his hand across his forehead again. "After that, she had her own key made. Started popping in whenever she wanted. Finally, refused to leave." He folded his arms and leaned back against the sofa. "She lectured me about how I should have been more assertive with you. What a joke. I found out she was tracking my movements twenty-four hours a day. You know how I loved that, don't you?"

"You could have ordered her out of the house." My God, why was she saying something that could set him off?

"Ordered her? Ha. I tried. It would have taken the sheriff to oust her. Can you see that plastered on the front page of the *Stone Harbor Journal*? I should have never got involved with her."

"No fooling," Katie thought without saying it. The last thing she needed was to upset him further.

Jeff's chin dropped to his chest; he stared at the floor. "Believe me, there was no telling Caroline to do anything. I gave her every chance to bow out gracefully."

"Every chance," Katie said, deciding to agree with anything he said from here on.

"The other day I was going to fly down to New York to see Robert and meet his new girlfriend. Caroline threw a fit. 'How could you make plans without me?' she bellowed. 'Why don't you bring the kids here to visit us?' As if I would bring any of them to the house with her there?" Jeff swirled his drink around in his glass. "She was trying to take over my life."

"Maybe you should have stayed in your new hotel suite in Barrington," Katie said, but wished at once that she hadn't broken her rule and said something else that could irritate him. Only deep down, Katie wondered if she was enjoying just a little bit hearing how Caroline made him squirm.

"Should I have handed over that beautiful house to her? I don't think so." He stretched his hands inside out, weaving his fingers together. "I gave her every opportunity to be a good sport."

"If you've kicked her out for good, Jeff, you won't have to worry about her anymore." She picked up her glass and pretended to sip the Scotch. "By the way, just when did you send her packing?"

"Before 8:00 a.m.," he said.

"You mean today?"

"Yes," he said. "She wandered into the bedroom and I told her I was going to drive to Boston today to see you. 'I'll make your life miserable if you do,' she said. 'You owe me. I helped you escape her.' Then she stuck her chin out and looked me straight in the face. 'You can't go,' she said."

He clenched his jaw. "That's when I told her to get the hell out and never come back." He pulled himself up on the sofa. "Believe me she scuttled out the door then. Like a scared rabbit."

"She's really gone then?"

He gave Katie an okay sign with his thumb and finger. "She's gone."

He poured more whiskey into his glass, took another swallow and gazed back at Katie through bleary eyes. "Listen, Katie. I want to be straight with you. Getting rid of her was more difficult than I've let on. Here's what actually happened. When I headed toward the door to leave she followed me screeching, 'If you go, you'll be sorry because I'm not budging from this house'."

He stirred the Scotch in his glass with his forefinger and then licked the finger. "That's when I told her she'd ruined my goddam life. And she shouted back, 'Your life isn't ruined. You're lucky to be rid of that self-centered woman.' Then she did her song and dance about how I'd never had a say in my marriage anyway.

"'You stupid woman!' I said. 'How did you ever get a PHD in psychology? You wanted to believe your own theories. I was never a co-dependent to Katie or anyone else.'"

"And that's when she left?"

His shaking was worse now; he had to hold his glass with both hands. "That's right," he mumbled.

"In that case, I don't see why we can't leave for Stone Harbor right now. I'll drive," she repeated.

He took hold of his jacket zipper again and ran it up and down a few times. "All the way here today I kept telling myself, 'Katie will be waiting for me at the other end'."

Katie gasped silently at this assumption, but pressed on. "It would be best for us to start out tonight."

"No," he said. "The more I think about it, the more I believe Caroline could have returned to the house. She still has her own key and I'm not up to dealing with her tonight." He set his glass down hard. Whiskey spurted up from the glass to the tabletop and dripped to the floor. "She claimed to know everything about me. She was an expert on what *you* did to rile me up, but she didn't get it herself." He gazed off as if he'd lost his train of thought, then made a fist and punched it into the palm of his other hand.

Katie flinched but tried to steady herself. "If she's back in the house, I'll help you get her out of there. Together we can shove her out the door if we have to." Katie was taken aback for a moment at her own advice – as if shoveling a woman out of her home were an ordinary occurrence.

He stared down at his shoes. "No. We can't do that." He went silent for a few seconds and then glanced around the living room. "You never did finish buying furniture for this place, did you?"

"I'll furnish it, I suppose." She wasn't going to let him deter her from the emergency at hand. "Well then, we could call a friend of Caroline's and ask him or her to come get her." Amazed again at her own ingenuity, Katie supposed it was a skill she'd perfected during their marriage. "When we force Caroline out, we can call a locksmith to change all the locks." She made herself keep talking, but her stomach muscles were pulling tighter with each of her own suggestions. *All I want is for him to step outside the condo and follow me through the lobby to the front door where our six foot four security officer is on duty.*

"No good," he said, this time lifting up the bottle to his mouth and drinking from the nozzle.

She'd never seen him swallow this amount of booze. Realizing his attitude toward her could change in an instant, she searched for something, anything to say to keep his interest. "I'll bet Caroline was outraged when she left. Was she carrying on something awful?"

"I don't know."

Katie yanked herself up in her chair. "You don't know?"

"I didn't actually see her leave." He lowered his voice. "I couldn't wait to get here. In the car I kept saying, 'Katie will help me. She won't turn me away.'"

"Help you what, Jeff?"

"Nothing. Just be here for me. Tonight of all nights."

Her chest grew heavier with each word he spoke. *God, please let me find a way to get him to leave.* "I still think we should go to the Stone Harbor house. If Caroline is there all alone and feeling anxious, you don't know what she might do."

Jeff jerked himself forward on the sofa and Katie feared she had finally pushed him too far. Quickly softening her voice, she said, "On the other hand, Jeff. If she's there we'll have a chance to settle this situation forever."

"I'm all strung out. I already told you I can't face her right now."

He picked up his bottle, studied it for a moment and then took another swig. "God damn woman!" he growled. "She's the one who told me that blowing off steam was healthy for a person."

He sloshed another gulp of whiskey down his throat and sputtered, "Up hers! Fucking witch! When I tried to get out the door a second time, she followed me aiming those piercing eyes of hers at me. 'You can't go to see Katie!' she yelled.

"Christ, Katie. Can you imagine how that pissed me off?"

No, Katie thought, because she couldn't imagine anyone getting in Jeff's face like that in the first place. His whole being must have been revved up at hearing Caroline's ultimatum. If Katie had been a voice inside Caroline's head she'd have screamed, *"Step back. Don't demand that Jeff do anything! It will only get worse. Get out of his way!"*

Katie raised her voice above the sound of her own pulse throbbing in her ears. "You must have been furious, Jeff," she said.

He balled his hand into a fist again. "All she had to do was back off and shut up. Be sensible. But no, she had to keep mouthing off. She could have been a nice contact in Stone Harbor. No harm done. We could have all ended up friends. Jesus, what a brainless bitch." He took another hearty swallow of whiskey from the bottle.

Without warning, a surge of nausea rolled over Katie, in waves, one after the other, not subsiding. She swiped her hand across her mouth and held it there without moving until she could speak again.

"Did you lose your temper, Jeff?" she asked him.

"Damn right," he said, tilting the bottle to his lips once more, only this time much of the amber liquid escaped the sides of his mouth and dripped down his chin. "Stubborn bulldog," he said. "She could have shut up and saved herself some trouble."

Something in the way Jeff suddenly sat up stiffly gripping the bottle, not letting his eyes meet hers, froze Katie in place. Under her sweater she felt the beating of her heart against her ribs. With the horror of an explosion the darkest possibility thundered through her brain, pushing at the edges of her skull. Weak and dizzy, she grabbed her belly with both arms crossed over it to counteract the stabbing pain in her gut. Perspiration slid down her spine and dripped between her breasts. Damp hair clung to the back of her neck.

She knew.

Katie knew.

"Caroline wasn't breathing when you left the house. Was she, Jeff?" she said.

"She wouldn't shut up."

"But you shut her up."

"I had to stop her yelping."

"And you had to hit her. And then hit her again, right, Jeff?"

"What the hell," he mumbled, then grimaced and brought the bottle to his mouth and sucked on the nozzle.

Katie watched him roll himself into the corner of the sofa with his lips around the neck of the bottle, knees pulled up and resting on his stomach.

"Is that what happened, Jeff?" she asked him.

He stopped sucking on the bottle and looked over at her with glazed eyes. In a voice almost inaudible, he said, "The last I know I was standing over her body on the bed. Then I looked down and saw a pillow clutched in my hand."

He seemed bewildered and settled back into the cushions.

Her own body as taut as she imagined Caroline's now lying on their bed, Katie said, "I understand, Jeff."

Neither spoke for a full minute until Katie asked, "Do you know what you did after that? Before leaving the house, Jeff?"

He shook his head back and forth. "I don't know if I do. I think I left your number on the answering machine." He rubbed his eyes. "I remember trying to make it look like a robbery. Busted the lock on my safe and tossed everything into a plastic bag. I hope it's in my car in your parking lot."

He sat up pulling his shoulders back. "And I got the hell out of there."

"Then we have to think," Katie said. *But think what?* All the thoughts being released in her own mind terrified her, nearly paralyzing her. She couldn't find her voice. In the worst of times, she had never thought Jeff capable of...But why not? *Remember he tried to choke you,* a voice inside her screamed, *This might have been me. This was supposed to be me.* Then, another thought overshadowed the rest: *I'm not safe. In the single tick of a clock, he could turn on me.* As if the oxygen to her windpipe had shut off, she suddenly felt herself slipping away into a black silent place. She fought for a breath until her surroundings and Jeff, who was still talking, came back into focus.

Trying to refocus on the immediate and what to do next, she asked, "Was Caroline on duty this weekend?"

Jeff slouched further into the sofa. "No, but someone will come looking for her when she isn't in her office on Monday." He pulled himself up and made a victory sign with two fingers and smiled for the first time all evening. "By then, of course, I'll be back in my office in Barrington."

He blew her another kiss. "You know, Katie, I was going to give you the robbery story too." He slapped his hand to his heart. "I should have known you'd understand. Shit, Katie you're as dependable as an old oak tree. A goddamn oak tree."

He got up from the sofa, stumbled over to her and with both arms lifted her up from her chair and pulled her tight to his chest. Then he snuggled his head into her shoulder and started to kiss her neck.

She tried to move but, with both of his arms around her, couldn't budge. He slid one hand under her sweater and began to caress her breasts. His other hand moved slowly from her neck down her back.

Knowing she couldn't push him away without arousing his anger, Katie dragged her arm up his torso to his face, brought a finger to his mouth and whispered, "Not yet."

He loosened his hold on her. "What do you mean?" he asked.

"Because I have to ask you something important first," she said. "Since you have my number on your answering machine I have to know what to say if someone calls here for you."

"Say I came here on Friday and stayed all weekend," he said and then lurched toward her again. Wrapping both of his arms around her, he bent down and rested his whiskey wet mouth on her lips and kissed her sloppily. Then he stepped back and touched her cheek. "A hell of a mess, Sweetheart," he said. "But we'll be fine now. Everything's under control. We'll get through this together."

She backed up a few inches. "Come with me," she said lifting his hand gently and guiding him down the hall to the bedroom.

"Please, stretch out on the bed, Jeff," she said. She untied his shoes and dropped them one at a time to the floor. Then she sat next to him and cradled his head onto a pillow. *I can do this,* she told herself. She moved her fingers tenderly over his cheeks and across his forehead. Brushing his hair back from his face, she recalled the very first time she had done that, and maybe the hundreds of times since then. She felt an old, old caring, as it was in the beginning, surfacing against her will, manufacturing tears in her throat and behind her eyes and assured herself that she would have the strength to do what was required.

She started to stand up but he grasped her arm and pulled her back into bed with him.

She snuggled up to his neck and whispered in his ear, "A few minutes can't matter. Let me get ready."

She took his face in her hands, brought her soft open lips to his mouth and kissed him. Then she slid off the bed. "I'll be right back," she said.

She went over to her bureau and lifted a black lace nightgown from a drawer and then turned on the nightstand radio, moving the dial to her soft rock station where Roberta Flack's sweet voice was singing "The first time ever I saw your face..." At the door with the nightgown over her arm, she looked back just as Jeff's lips formed the words, "I love you."

"Me too," she answered.

He lifted his head up from the pillow. "Hurry back, Katie. Please."

She walked down the hall, opened the bathroom door and flipped on a light, then continued on to the kitchen, reached for the wall telephone, and steadying her hand, dialed 911.

Chapter Twenty

Seated together in the front row of the Providence Rhode Island Superior Courtroom, Katie and the children waited anxiously for the proceedings to begin. Mathew, Tommy and Martha had taken time off from school for the trial but Robert, who had somehow managed to blame Katie for his dad's crime, had refused to join them. Katie darted a quick glance at the defense table where Jeff and his attorneys had just assembled. She was taken aback immediately by Jeff's calm demeanor. He appeared unaffected by the flurry of activity at the other side of the room where the chief prosecutor, a confident looking gray-haired man, was furiously sorting through a stack of papers pertaining to a case the media had already dubbed a "slam dunk".

Katie decided that Jeff's serenity stemmed from his ability to rationalize his own behavior. He is most likely convinced his actions will be understood once the jury learns how he was provoked beyond endurance by Caroline, Katie imagined. When Martha questioned her dad's odd behavior, Katie answered, "I guess he must be confident he won't be convicted." Later in the day, however, Jeff appeared every bit as uninvolved when his own defense attorneys introduced their "temporary insanity" argument.

On the morning of the third day, Katie worked up a bad case of tremors in the prosecutors' office after hearing she would be called to testify that afternoon. Luckily, the moment she was ushered to the witness stand by a court officer, a certain coolness settled over her. She answered the prosecutor's and the defense attorney's questions without hesitation, relating events leading up to the crime and to Jeff's confession to her of the murder itself. Though she kept her eyes straight ahead on the attorney questioning her, she could feel the cut of Jeff's glare throughout her testimony.

As soon as she was returned to the prosecutors' office she gasped with relief and then congratulated herself: *I didn't crumple like an accordion. I didn't run hysterically from the courtroom. It's over!* She cupped her hands to her mouth and let her head drop onto her chest. Later the prosecutor came back to his office and complimented her on her confident and rational performance and she shrugged, "I think I was too exhausted to be dramatic. Strange though, the whole time I was in the witness chair I felt as though I was viewing myself from the back of the courtroom while listening to someone else's voice. I think that helped more than anything."

Throughout the rest of the trial Katie and the children drank coffee and Cokes and ate egg or tuna salad sandwiches from a refrigerator in a refreshment shop in the basement of the courthouse. To keep up their spirits they resurrected stories from the past few years, embarrassing moments, mimicking each other's friends, teasing one another, anything that could make them smile and divert their attention from the tragedy that was playing out in the courtroom. Then on the fifth, and what would be the last day of the trial, Katie took a long cold drink from her Coke and prayed out loud for all of them: "I hope we can survive this experience with some dignity intact and the energy to hope for a better future. I know if I am able to do that it will be due to the help I've received from other people, the three of you and my family and your mom's phone calls to all of us every night and my good pal Natalie – *and most of all to Steve, my sweet friend and confidant, for being at my side throughout this awful ordeal,* she added in silence.

Katie thoughts drifted off for a few minutes until they were suddenly interrupted by Martha who had begun to cry and then sob uncontrollably. Katie, who had never once in the years she had known Martha, seen her shed a tear, seemed paralyzed at first by this astonishing event. By the time she reached her hand out to the girl, Martha had dropped her head to the table and was wailing into her own folded arms.

Katie leaped up from her own chair, bent over Martha and ran her fingers through Martha's long sandy blonde hair. "Just get it out, honey. At last," she urged. "Let go of all those emotions you've stifled your entire young life." When she glanced over at a speechless Mathew and Tommy across the table from her she saw that both boys were brushing tears from their cheeks with the backs of their hands. "This is good. Good for all of us," Katie blurted out recalling for herself the many times Mathew had insisted, "I'm great" and Tommy had flashed a smile and given her an okay sign with his finger and thumb and Martha had stuck her chin in the air stating, "I'm fine. I'm always fine" when nothing was great or okay or fine at all.

Just then a bell rang summoning them back to the courtroom because the jury, after only five hours' deliberation had agreed to a verdict. Katie and the kids rushed back to their places in the front row. Sliding silently onto the wooden bench each of them reached for the hand next to them. Standing behind the table next to his young, exquisitely dressed attorney, Jeff stared blankly into the dead air ahead of him. Katie could hear the pounding of her own heart as the jury foreperson handed a piece of paper to the court officer who gave it to the judge. The judge instructed the foreperson to read the verdict aloud. "Guilty on the charge of second degree murder," was all that Katie heard until a moment later the judge began to speak again and she realized that he was about to pronounce Jeff's sentence immediately.

"Twenty-five years to life," the judge stated clearly with a deep firm voice. "With no parole."

A second later, Jeff, still standing, whirled around and aimed his squinted, accusing eyes at Katie in the front row. Then he howled in a booming voice that seemed to bounce off the dome ceiling and echo from every corner of the courtroom: "You back stabbing Judas. You caused all of this – start to finish. You never listen! I told you everything was under control! You tricked me! You fucking stupid ass bitch!" Then he fell backwards into his chair and pounded both fists on the defense table. Two court officers burst in from a side door and dove at him, grabbed his hands, handcuffed him from behind and dragged him struggling and still yelling from the Providence Superior Courtroom.

"I decided last night that I need to get away by myself for a few weeks. I'm going to drive cross-country to California," Katie told Steve and Natalie and the children the day after the trial had ended. They were all having lunch together in a Boston restaurant and Katie had silenced the group with her plan. She had realized the night before that every cell of her body was bone tired and that her brain was fried and that she was incapable of making good decisions.

Getting only blank stares in response to her declaration of major fatigue and her self-proclaimed recovery plan, she asked them to please understand. "In this condition I would make bad errors in judgment and I've already made enough dumb stupid mistakes for two lifetimes. My life has gone up in smoke. I have to figure out who the heck I am now."

"I think it's a good idea," Martha said. "Go get your head straight, Katie."

"Do it," Mathew said. "It's been an ugly trip for all of us the past few months."

Tommy smiled. "It's a fantastic idea if you'll take me with you."

Katie leaned back in her chair and let her mind wander a moment thinking: *I need to see acres of Iowa corn in full bloom. And be hypnotized by an endless strip of Nebraska road stretching straight ahead as the crow flies. And to lick the taste of a dry, hot Wyoming wind from my lips. And when I reach San Francisco, I need to have some long overdue conversations with Maxine and rest of my old pals.*

"Oh, of course, I have to come back to settle my affairs. I can't seem to focus beyond that though," she added. "I don't know. I just don't know..."

Steve shook his head. "I think you must know what my reaction is to this sudden road trip plan. I guess you have to do what you have to do, though. When are you leaving?"

"Day after tomorrow," she said.

She was going to say more but Steve cut her off. He threw his arms up in the air. "Day after tomorrow? I give up. Send me a postcard of the Golden Gate Bridge, will you?"

"Oh, Steve, I was hoping we could have a good talk tonight."

Steve turned away from her without a reply and Natalie said, "I hope you find your answers somewhere along the way. But tell me you're not going to chug coast to coast in that old broken down Chevy."

"No, I'm donating it to the Smithsonian. Think I'm going to buy a shiny bronze Camero."

"Cool," Tommy roared.

In front of the restaurant Steve opened her car door. "Keep safe. If you have time, let me know you're alive."

She reached for his hand and gave it a squeeze. "Please understand, Steve. I have to do this." She dropped into the driver's seat as Steve backed away from the car and waved.

"*Why should Steve understand another of my requests,*" she asked herself. *Expecting him to appreciate my need to take this trip is asking too much.* She grasped her hands tighter to the steering wheel admitting: *I don't want to hurt him again, I really don't. I know Steve's welfare will be tugging at my heart throughout this trip. And yet, I can't seem to make a U-turn and go back to the restaurant.*

* * * * * * *

In spite of her distress at leaving without Steve's blessing, Katie looked forward to revisiting her old life in California. Feeling more refreshed each day of her five day cross country journey though, she suddenly became apprehensive as she approached Maxine's bungalow in Berkeley. How would Maxine look and how much will she have changed, she wondered. Would they have as much in common as they had in the past?

But, all her concerns evaporated the minute Maxine flew from her front door and ran down the drive to meet Katie's car. Her long blonde hair still fell freely at her back but the gypsy skirt and peasant blouse had been replaced by cargo pants and a cotton shirt. Nevertheless, she sensed that this was her friend, basically unchanged.

She and Maxine fell easily into a four-day non-stop conversation that continued from morning coffee at Maxine's kitchen table to afternoon shopping, then on through dinner in San Francisco with former co-workers and old anti-war buddies at their old favorite Union Street pub – always finishing up back in Berkeley over a bottle of wine with Maxine's affable, urbane, good natured husband Tony filling the glasses.

A week later, on the morning she was to leave, Katie said a difficult goodbye to Maxine. Her friend, still bursting with plans to improve society and now excessively in love with Tony had thank goodness had *enough caring left over for me, letting me moan over Jeff one minute and damn him the next – over and over again.*

"Come back as soon as you can," Maxine said tossing Katie's suitcase into the backseat of her car. "I'm sure *New Times* would hire you back on the spot if they thought you were available. Not sure you could buy another Pacific Heights flat for the amount you received for yours a few years ago, but we could find something smaller that you could afford." Then Maxine laughed. "And I could use your help here again. We never run out of causes to champion and evil to protest." She sighed. "Don't listen to me or anyone else, Katie, just do what's good for you."

"I hope I will know what that is this time. I'll keep in touch better from now on. Promise," Katie cried out from her car window as she drove off.

* * * * * * *

While passing Sacramento and climbing the Sierras, Katie reflected on her wonderful time with Maxine, but then had to acknowledge her one disappointment. She realized early in the visit that she'd been unable to describe properly what she'd been through the past few years. Not what it was like to *live* the events, what it *felt* like at the time, what lasting effect she knew they would have on her. She loved Maxine as much as ever but accepted that she would never know how it had *really been back there – in that plac*e. Katie wondered if her inability to give Maxine true *understanding* of her experiences might resemble the frustration of war veterans who try in vain to relate to loved ones or old friends the horrors they've survived in some godforsaken hellish place and how much they've been changed by them.

On the open road with plenty of uninterrupted time, Katie drifted back to the day an attractive Irish American sauntered into her life. No denying it, she was smitten with him immediately. How was he able to do that, she still asked herself. She believed it was far more than chemistry: *It had to be*, she thought. *I'd have dealt with that without falling in love. There was a strong physical attraction all right, but I really thought the man "understood" me...I truly did.* He encouraged me to fess up to my deepest fears, all those vulnerabilities that I'd kept inside before he prodded them out of me. He listened intently to my stories about a dismissive father who'd ignored me no matter how many new tap dancing steps and perfect cartwheels I performed for him or straight A report cards I brought home. Oh, how entranced Jeff seemed by my childhood confessions!

One afternoon at the highest point of the Colorado Rocky Mountains, as close to God as she'd ever been, Katie admitted to herself how easily she'd been seduced by Jeff's feigned interest in her childhood. And she swore on every mountain peak surrounding her: *I am going to acknowledge that Jeff was not being compassionate or caring even during our courtship. And that with carefully contrived patience and concern, he was merely soaking up all that background information to win me over and manipulate me later.*

And I played a part in Jeff's duplicity, Katie conceded for the first time. She shifted uncomfortably in her driver's seat. Yes, *I'd been pleased to replace my father's unrequited love with Jeff's grand promises. Done so willingly, even gratefully. And stubbornly refused to believe that Jeff had loved me as much as he was capable of loving anyone. I so wanted to trust that he had much more love to give. But there had never been a great reservoir of love waiting to be released at some undisclosed date. He had already given what he had to give. And it was so little after all.*

Somewhere on a stretch of Iowa corn fields along Highway 80, Katie made the decision to finish work on the second issue of *Moving On* in Boston. She pulled into a roadside gas station to fill up her tank and bought a cold Coke from a soda machine. Suddenly brimming with an eagerness she hadn't experienced in months, she hopped back into her sparkly new Camero and clicked on the radio. She punched in a good R&B station, turned up the volume, and headed eastward again, four windows open all the way.

Sliding gratefully into a more pleasant memory, Katie recalled the day a month earlier when her divorce from Jeff had become final. She and Steve had honored the milestone together at the Catch of the Day pub. While sitting beside one another in a booth Steve reminded her, "I told you I'd be waiting for you at the finish line. Well here I am as promised." Katie turned to kiss his hand that was resting on her shoulder.

"I love you, woman," Steve whispered to her. He set down his glass, placed one hand under her chin and kissed her on the cheek. "Actually this is not quite the finish line, though, is it?" he added. "I know the only thing on your mind now is that disgusting trial. But pencil me in on your calendar the day after that, please."

Remembering this now, Katie envisioned – as she had been during the entire trip – Steve's reaction at lunch the day she revealed her plan to take this trip. "I'm so sorry to have hurt him one more time," she confessed in a whisper to her empty car. "I must have been desperate for some time to myself. I will beg him, at the very least, to accept my heartfelt apology."

On impulse, the next afternoon she ignored the Expressway Exit sign for Boston and continued straight ahead. Later that afternoon she drove into Barrington Village as she had hundreds of times before and yet somehow it felt different, the sun on the pavement warmer, the ocean breeze more noticeable and refreshing than she remembered. With trembling fingers she punched in Steve's phone number at the *Gazette* on her car phone.

Caught off guard and then speechless for a moment, Steve sputtered, "Katie, for God's sake, where are you?"

"I just arrived in Barrington," she said. "Can you meet me at the Catch? I'll be there in ten minutes."

Feeling anxious suddenly she wished she'd changed into something less disgusting than the khaki driving gear that she'd worn for the past couple of days on the road. But her jitters disappeared the second she saw Steve waiting for her at the entrance of their pub. She parked, flung open her car door and ran to him. He threw his arms around her, lifted her off her feet and locked her in his arms. "Well, damn, with no word from you I figured once you set foot in California I might never see you again."

"I don't blame you," she answered and through a burst of tears asked, "Can we go inside and talk?"

They found a back booth and sat down next to one another. "I don't know where to start. I have so much to say. I've screwed up my life for so long, Steve. What a fool I've been. I tried to save a marriage that was doomed from the start. I listened to a weary old voice in my head yapping about the sanctity of marriage no matter what. And my compulsion not to fail, ever, at anything. That left me believing I had a duty to make everything turn out right." She stopped and turned to face him. "How could I have ignored all the normal self-survival instincts for as long that were all but slapping me in the face with red flags?"

Steve placed a hand over her mouth tenderly. "I've known all along what was driving you. Trying to be Miss Perfect in your own far from perfect world. I know you, Katie. I've been impatient but feeling powerless all this time watching you try to grow roses in a goddamn desert," he said.

They were interrupted by the waitress long enough for Steve to order two martinis. Then he put his arm around Katie and brought her head to his shoulder. They only moved when the waitress returned with their drinks and then he toasted Katie: "This is right, Katie. You and me. Has been all along."

"I have an incredible nerve asking you for anything at this point," she said. "I at least wanted to apologize."

"But you knew I'd come when you called me today."

"No I didn't but I had to find out. I thought about you while I was away, even suddenly while midstream in conversation with old friends. I am able to embrace now what I couldn't while with Jeff constantly trying to negotiate over one thing and another." She hesitated and then turned to look into his eyes. "But I've loved you all this time. I know too that I've never really been in love before you. Not like this – so completely and unafraid, with no reservations."

"Do you know how long I've waited to hear you say that?" He took her face in his hands and kissed her lips. "I've loved you every day since the day we met."

"We've wasted so much time. All my fault. I'm so sorry for what I've put you through."

He brought her hand to his lips and kissed it. "What do you say we waste no more time on blame or regrets?"

"Let's drink to that," she said smiling and clinking her glass against his.

They took a few more sips of their drinks and Katie put down her glass. "Let's get out of here," she said.

He reached for her hand immediately and said, "Now."

On their way to Steve's car they stopped near the ocean's edge and he cradled her in his arms. She reached up and brushed her lips softly against his.

Engulfing her in his arms this time he held her close to his chest and they kissed eagerly and passionately for the first time.

"Come home with me," Steve said.

"Oh, yes. And when I get there I'm going to pull the drapes and lock the door and shut off the phone," she whispered in his ear.

"Katie, we are going to get to know each other now, finally, really know each other in every way there is to know another person. That's a promise, my love."

"And I'll keep you to it," she answered laughing and grasping onto his hand as they dashed through the parking lot together toward his car.